WAKE UP

—— TO ——

SHAKE UP

MORNING GET UP

CASEY CHINEDU IFEDI

Published by Victorious You Press™
Charlotte NC, USA

Unless otherwise indicated, scripture quotations are from the Holy Bible, King James Version. All rights reserved.

TITLE: WAKE UP TO SHAKE UP

First Printed: 2023

Cover Designer: Nadia Monsano

Editor: Amanda Smith

ISBN: 978-1-952756-97-9

ISBN: (ebook) 978-1-952756-98-6

Printed in the United States of America

For details email joan@victoriousyoupress.com

or visit us at www.victoriousyoupress.com

ACKNOWLEDGEMENTS

Special thanks to The Almighty God, The Ifedi Empire, and everyone that has contributed to making this book a success. Thanks to all who have contributed to the success of our organization.

TABLE OF CONTENT

INTRODUCTION

A Life Guide: A Motivational and Mission-Focused Tool and Resource. Rise and Grind.

Welcome to the four "M" Movement where we maximize your money, motivation, and mission.

A Global Financial Literacy for All Movement (FLFL) Publication.

- TheGeneralspeaks™ platform was created to encourage, motivate, and inspire individuals to become a better version of themselves through education, exercise, investing, and an overall holistic approach. My desire is for you to implement practical strategies to improve your daily life.

- TheGeneralspeaks™- a consulting, coaching, and investing platform aimed at holistically improving life.

I Live Purpose. I Speak Life.

Sponsored and supported by The T.E.A.M. Incorporated

The T.E.A.M. (Talented, Empowered, Aspired, Men) Incorporated was created to empower men of color worldwide. To date, we have helped over 650 men of color graduate and matriculate successfully into society.

With a 100 percent graduation rate, we are positioned to rewrite the narrative of men of color from all over the world. We will rewrite our story, our way!

MAXIMIZE YOUR MONEY

Work to Learn How Money Works

January 1, 2023

The more you learn, the more you'll earn.

When building a financial foundation, consider this formula: money (+) time and rate of return (-) inflation and taxes (=) wealth. If you're not making money, you're losing money. And, while we should all strive to build a savings, it's better to spend money that's left after saving, rather than saving what's left after spending.

Investing is another component to building wealth, but learning to invest effectively, takes time.

~ 1 ~

Wake Up Action Step: Save at least 15-20 percent of your income and use the money saved to invest. Significant financial growth does not happen at the saving level; it happens when you invest. Once you learn to invest, you'll begin to see a return on your investments.

Maintain the Needs and Decrease the Wants

January 2, 2023

To maintain the needs and decrease the wants, you must understand what essentials are needed, and which are not. When you stop spending money on items you want and don't need, you'll dramatically improve your financial outlook. Lifestyle and spending habits can affect one's financial stability, so try to be conscious of your spending. In fact, purchasing discounted items can still be costly when budgeting and building financial wealth is your end goal.

~ 2 ~

Wake Up Action Step: Creating a simple budget, tracking your spending and your expenses are ways you can maintain your needs and decrease the wants. Consider setting a weekly schedule to monitor and review your business and bank accounts.

Money is a Mindset

January 3, 2023

How you manage your money could potentially determine if you're blessed with more opportunities. Saving and spending habits are a learned behavior, so to increase financial literacy within a family or a community, one should know how money works. Gradual change over an extended period can dramatically change a person's life. One year can really make a difference.

~ 3 ~

Wake Up Action Step: Write out any expenses you can cut out. Create a list of areas that may be holding you back, so you can prepare to move forward into financial abundance.

Time over Money

January 4, 2023

We've all heard the saying, "time is money," and many people tend to believe this. However, time is exponentially more valuable than money. Consider this narrative: if someone handed you a bag that contained one million dollars and said you can have it, but under one condition...you give up your life. Would you execute the contract? Why or why not? Many would choose to not compromise their life for what's essentially, pieces of paper. Time is the one resource that once exhausted, can never be redeemed. Use the money but invest your time.

~ 4 ~

Wake Up Action Step: Pay yourself after each pay period by saving 15-20 percent. By doing so, you'll start building your emergency fund and investment account. Build, build, and build some more. Also, remember these two words: invest and progress.

Invest Well. Invest and Progress

January 5, 2023

While you should strive to work hard and put your best foot forward, learning to work smarter will help you invest well. Create and implement a game plan that will help you save, as well as build capital. Capital saved is important, but capital invested properly, is supreme. Think of your money like little soldiers. You can deploy them in the market at any time. However, knowing when and where to invest your assets can place you in a position to succeed or fail.

~ 5 ~

Wake Up Action Step: Investing is a mindset. The best time to invest was 20 years ago, but you can start investing right now. Choose two or three areas and/or industries to invest your income. And while diversifying your portfolio is important, understanding your investments is essential to becoming a successful investor.

Build Wealth That Will Last

January 6, 2023

Steady and consistent accumulation of saved funds is the most powerful way to create and maintain wealth. Building a solid foundation will take time, but if it's easily and quickly built, the easier it may be to tear down. Fortify your foundation by investing properly and effectively. Avoid any get rich quick schemes and be disciplined in your actions. Understand the mission at hand and don't underestimate the power of financial literacy and financial freedom. In a capitalist world, it's impossible to be truly free without capital.

~ 6 ~

Wake Up Action Step: Write out your financial goals. Be open and honest with yourself when discussing your personal finances. Ask yourself, where are you currently in your finances? Where would you like to be financially in five years?

The Power of Compound Interest

January 7, 2023

Compound interest is the interest earned on your interest. Use the rule of 72 to calculate the effects of compound interest. To find how long it will take to double your money, take 72 and divide it by the rate of return. Understanding how compound interest works and how it can affect your investments is important when building long term wealth.

~ 7 ~

Wake Up Action Step: Take time to understand compound interest. Learn how it works and how to use it to your advantage. Start by researching compound interest and finding out how it's used to yield effective results.

Learners are Earners

January 8, 2023

Ultimately, there are two types of people when it comes to building wealth...those who don't understand the way money works and must work hard for their money, and those who do understand how money works, so they let the money work for them. Which one are you?

Wealthy people have taken the time to learn and understand how money works. However, wealthy people don't know everything when it comes to financial freedom, so they seek experts who can advise them on a particular matter.

Now's the time, to learn more, earn more, and increase the rate of return.

~ 8 ~

Wake Up Action Step: Today, decide if you will be a learner and an earner. Stop making excuses and start learning how to manage your personal finances. Your financial freedom is up to you, so when you have no plan to save and invest, you're setting yourself up to fail.

Invest in the Interest

January 9, 2023

Don't underestimate the power of interest. Interest that compounds can be an asset, or a liability. Debt that carries compound interest can be a liability, but that's depending on how the debt is leveraged. Without a financial game plan to leverage the debt, one could be paying a monthly balance each month without making any real impact on the actual principal. Simple interest will grow slower if it does not compound. Compound interest is where the magic happens. Invest in the interest.

~ 9 ~

Wake Up Action Step: Understand the kind of interest you are investing in - leveraging the correct interest, with the right investing vehicle. Combining the two can be a game changer financially. Start investing today!

Rate of Return

January 10, 2023

Rate of return is the percentage change in value of an investment. Did you make or lose money on the investment? This is what the annual rate of return of an investment will help determine. If you put $100.00 into an investment with an annual interest rate of 10 percent, your gross will be $110.00. With this same investment, if you add a 3 percent taxation with inflation at 4 percent, you will net 3 percent interest on top of the initial investment. Your overall return would be $103.00. The major takeaway is to understand rate of return and how it'll affect your overall return on each investment.

~ 10 ~

Wake Up Action Step: Study the rate of return before you invest. Take time today to understand the overall rate of return on each investment vehicle. No one can save for you, so start saving and investing yourself today. When you save and invest, you'll begin to see a major change in your financial security.

Inflate in Real Life

January 11, 2023

Inflation is the rate of increase in prices over a period of time. Everything is going up. Gas prices are up. The cost of milk and eggs are up...but what about your life? Is the value you bring to the marketplace going up as well? Has your mindset or skill set gone up? Look around you, things are inflating higher every day. What about you? Are you vibrating higher? Poverty chases Money. Money chases Wealth. Wealth chases Value. Inflate in real life.

~ 11 ~

Wake Up Action Step: Inflation typically occurs when a country prints more money than it earns. When this happens, everyone loses. The value of the currency is depreciated. Compound interest, the rate of return, inflation, and taxes are all things that are working against you.

Taxes, Our Biggest Expense

January 12, 2023

For many Americans, the largest expense over a lifetime is taxes. Most money generating activity requires taxation. It is impossible to build true wealth without learning and understanding how taxes work.

There is property tax, state tax, federal income tax, estate tax, and sales tax. Taxes can take as much as 40 percent of your yearly net earnings. This percentage can fluctuate depending on the administration in power.

~ 12 ~

Wake Up Action Step: Start today to learn and leverage the tax code. When you make money, you will be taxed. When you spend money, you will be taxed. When you save money, you will be taxed. Even when you die you will be taxed.

Capital to Gain

January 13, 2023

Capital gains are the increase in a capital asset's value and is realized when the asset is sold. Capital gains can be applied to any type of asset. This may include investments and those purchased for personal use. Gain can be short term (one year or less) or long term (more than one year). Capital gains are also taxed. Personal assets and/or investments may be considered capital assets. Personal homes, certificates of deposit (CDs), and stocks are all considered capital assets.

~ 13 ~

Wake Up Action Step: Learn how to leverage. The longer you hold an asset, the less taxes are owed on that particular asset. Start acquiring assets today. Consider holding on to assets for a longer period. Remember, taxes are typically the largest expense.

Build to Last

January 14, 2023

To build for the long term, you must plan for the road ahead. Not everyone will work forever, even if they do love their job/career. It's important to create a retirement plan that's sustainable and can protect your work and effort. With the life expectancy increasing by the year, the amount needed for retirement is also increasing. Building wealth is the key to building a life that will last.

~ 14 ~

Wake Up Action Step: Either you're planning to succeed or you're planning to fail. An individual that refuses to plan, has ultimately planned for the latter. Building wealth and saving for retirement is simply a game of numbers. Plan today for the tomorrow you desire to live. The choice is yours!

The Wealth Strategy

January 15, 2023

Failure is inevitable without a strategy. Use a tried and tested formula for wealth accumulation. Time (+) money (+/-) rate of return (-) inflation and taxes (=) wealth.

Use these seven tips for wealth accumulation:

a. Earn and make the money

b. Save the money and spend less

c. Invest the money while allowing the interest to compound to build and grow wealth

d. Invest the money into financial vehicles with a rate of return higher than inflation

e. Leverage your time. Start investing and growing money as soon as possible f. Find an investment that has tax advantages

g. Embrace your retirement season

If you follow these steps, you'll eventually begin to enjoy the fruits of your labor.

~ 15 ~

Wake Up Action Step: Don't try to recreate the wheel. There's no time for wasted time and energy. Consolidate your efforts into a singular wealth strategy and plan. Start by implementing these winning strategies today to start building wealth.

Wealth Build Up

January 16, 2023

Most people start off with little to no money. However, as one starts to save and properly invest, they'll eventually see a built up of wealth. There's an upward trend of wealth accumulation. Analyze where you are in your saving journey and learn and work to grow your current network. It's safe to say if you start saving and investing today, there's likely a higher chance of financial freedom versus someone who doesn't save or invest. Nothing is truly guaranteed, but we know and understand there are factors that influence the likelihood of certain results.

~ 16 ~

Wake Up Action Step: Be honest with yourself. There's no one to blame for the lack of financial prosperity. Yes, we may be disadvantaged in some way or another, but the biggest advantage for everyone, is time. No one truly knows how much time they have here on earth. The best way to predict the future is to create it.

Control Your Debt or Debt Will Control You

January 17, 2023

Whatever you refuse to manage, you'll manage to lose. Debt management is key. Debt is like a cancer that robs a person from future wealth accumulation. Debt can control your life if it's not properly managed. Debt can rob someone of their joy and happiness, and freedom. No one is truly free until they are financially free.

One keyway to reduce debt is to live below your means. Overspending is financially irresponsible, so buy things you need instead of things you want. Management is the major key.

~ 17 ~

Wake Up Action Step: Limit your credit card usage. Using a credit card is not bad but try to use it only when necessary. Make a list of all your debt. Use the snowball effect and start paying off the lowest balance first. Use the excess money from clearing one debt and roll that money over into your larger debt. Start small but be sure to start today to tackle your debt. It's on you!

Insure and Invest

January 18, 2023

Insurance is a means of protection from financial loss. This is a form of risk management, primarily used to hedge against the risk of a contingent or uncertain loss.

Investment is the dedication of an asset to attain an increase in value over a period of time. Investments require a sacrifice of some present asset, such as time, money, or effort.

Combine these two principles into your daily financial game plan. Investing is like playing offense and insurance is like playing defense. Good defense is good, but without good offense it may be difficult to win.

~ 18 ~

Wake Up Action Step: Look to see if you have an insurance policy. Be sure to invest in insurance. The purpose of investing is to generate a return from the invested asset. If structured correctly, a life insurance policy can be leveraged as a financial vehicle that can grow over time. Start building wealth today.

Multiply Your Life

January 19, 2023

Many people chase money. To position yourself for a more abundant life, you must learn how to increase the value you bring to the market. Growing and multiplying money is important. Being able to protect and keep money is also important.

There are four key areas to consider when determining how much life insurance is needed. The four areas include: expenses, annual income, housing, and education.

When calculating expenses make sure you include current, past, and future expenses. Annual income is the total amount of income produced on a yearly basis. Multiply annual income by ten. Education should also include any and every interest that may have incurred. Combine these four areas to determine the right amount of insurance you might need.

~ 19 ~

Wake Up Action Step: Multiply your mindset. Use today to write down the total amount in each of the four areas that impact the life insurance amount. Understand that protecting your assets is just as important as acquiring them. Start multiplying today!

An Indexed Life

January 20, 2023

Indexation means a price, wage, or other value based on the changes in another price or composite indicator of prices. Indexation can be done to adjust for the effects of inflation, the cost of living, input prices over time, or to adjust for different prices and costs in different geographical areas. Indexed growth is capped at a certain rate. Inversely, there is a 0 percent floor for all losses. Learn to build a useful and productive life. Leverage your assets and mitigate risk.

~ 20 ~

Wake Up Action Step: Use what you have to get what you want. Calculate your risk prior to investing. Write out a list of your investments and think through all possible losses. Put measures in place to control all current and future losses.

Live a Universal Life

January 21, 2023

Universal life insurance is a type of permanent life insurance. With a universal life policy, the insured person is covered for the duration of their life if they pay premiums and fulfill any other requirements of their policy to maintain coverage. Plan to live a fully insured life. Tomorrow isn't promised. The best way to determine the future is to plan it. Aggressively save and invest. A permanent strategy to insure a well-balanced and protected life is to pay the price by saving and investing today.

~ 21 ~

Wake Up Action Step: Start saving and investing into your future today. There's a winning strategy for life. Grow and protect your money. Use what the winners use.

Become the Key Person

January 22, 2023

Key person insurance is a life insurance policy that a company gets on a top executive or another critical individual. This insurance is needed if that person's death would be devastating to the future of the company. No matter the organization or company, there's always a key person that adds a supreme amount of value. The more you are paid, the more responsibility you are given. Embrace your responsibility. Leverage any and every position to become the highest version of yourself today.

~ 22 ~

Wake Up Action Step: Take one action step daily to position yourself to be a leader. Write out the life goals you wish to accomplish. Underneath each goal, write one task you'll commit to, at least once daily to help you achieve that goal.

Live a Life of Execution and Growth

January 23, 2023

Execution is having the power to put plans, actions, or laws into effect. An executive is the person or branch of a government responsible for putting policies or laws into effect. Phenomenal execution is respected and admired by all. Practice execution daily. Execution leads to growth and improvement. Life insurance for executives is typically paid by the company. The company pays the premium and can deduct it as a tax-exempt contribution. The benefit will go to the employee of the company. Executive policies have cash value that can be borrowed against.

~ 23 ~

Wake Up Action Step: Practice execution daily. Write out 3-5 tasks you plan to execute. For each task completed, draw a line, and write the word executed.

Live a Life of Execution and Growth: Part 2

January 24, 2023

Execution and growth are a choice. To maximize your life, one must learn execution and growth.

Executive life insurance policies may have cash value built up over time and loans can be taken out against the policy. Premium payments must be claimed as regular income. The family of the executive will receive the benefit. Position yourself to receive the very best life has to offer.

~ 24 ~

Wake Up Action Step: Track your progress and compare yourself against your yesterday. Ask yourself, how can I improve today?

Insurance Is Final

January 25, 2023

The idea we'll live forever is not practical or realistic. There are only two things almost guaranteed in life, death, and taxes. Taxes are guaranteed even when someone pays them for you.

Planners are winners, so it's wise to plan for the inevitable. Insure and work towards a life of productivity and purpose. Final expense insurance is a whole life insurance policy, specifically marked to cover the expenses associated with a funeral, memorial service, reception, cremation and/or burial. It's also commonly known as burial insurance, funeral insurance, or cremation insurance.

~ 25 ~

Wake Up Action Step: Those who don't qualify for life insurance, may use final expense insurance. Write out how much you'll need to cover your final expenses. Decide today you'll be an asset to your loved ones and not a liability.

Become a Living Benefit

January 26, 2023

Work to become an asset to everyone around you. Create insurance in your life by working consistently to improve your skill sets. Life insurance was created to protect a person's estate, business, and family. It allows you, the policy owner, to build cash value through your life insurance policy, which accumulates over your lifetime. This is considered a living benefit of life insurance. In contrast to a death benefit that pays out when you pass away, you can use the money while you're still alive.

~ 26 ~

Wake Up Action Step: Work to improve your emotional stability. Work to improve your mental and psychological well-being. Write out the ways you can become more of an asset to yourself and others.

Become a Living Benefit: Part 2

January 27, 2023

Accelerate your life with planned and focused action. Structure your life in a way you can leverage benefits while you're still living. Utilize life insurance with living benefits. Living benefits are also known as accelerated death benefits. Accelerated death benefits is a feature where the insurance company pays or advances a portion of the policy's death benefit to the insured to pay for care or treatment. If the insured dies, the balance of the death benefit will then be paid to the beneficiary.

~ 27 ~

Wake Up Action Step: Accelerate your life through planned and focused action. Write out three goals that'll move you towards your life's goals.

Become a Living Benefit: Part 3

January 28, 2023

Start today to create the life you want. Strategically invest in areas that will yield profit and return. There are some diseases that can financially cripple the future of many individuals. With illnesses such as heart disease, stroke, cancer, paralysis, and terminal illnesses with a diagnosis of less than 12 months to live, accelerated payments will be useful for the insured and their family.

~ 28 ~

Wake Up Action Step: Life insurance with living benefits can be more flexible and can provide needed cash, at critical times. Use today to apply for proper life insurance. Do not wait until it's too late. Your legacy may depend on it.

Life and Taxes

January 29, 2023

There are two things that are certain, death and taxes. The unique advantage of life insurance is that both of those areas can be addressed within a life policy.

In the event the insured dies, the entire death benefit including the cash value is income-tax free to the beneficiary. The gains within policy are not taxed. Earnings are tax deferred until the policy is surrendered, lapsed, or distributed. Plan your life while leveraging the tax advantages of a properly structured life policy.

~ 29 ~

Wake Up Action Step: Leverage what you have today. Write out the things in your life you have that can be used to improve your life today. Take an honest inventory of your life. What are ways you can improve? Work towards your highest version today.

Life and Taxes: Part 2

January 30, 2023

Another important tax advantage of a life insurance policy is the ability to withdraw cash value, tax free. When there is enough cash value within the policy, the premiums paid into the policy can be taken out tax free. Money can also be taken out of the policy outside of the premiums paid through a tax-free loan. The tax-free loan has a low net effective rate. When a loan is taken out against the policy, the insurance company will take the same amount of the loan from the cash value and transfer it to a loan reserve account. There will be interest charged on the loan.

~ 30

Wake Up Action Step: Put in the work today for the life you want tomorrow. Position yourself to borrow against the sweat equity you have invested. Build real value through premium and optimum energy and effort.

Life and Taxes: Part 3

January 31, 2023

Those who are wealthy understand and utilize the power of life insurance when building and protecting wealth long-term. Keep in mind, the tax advantages of life insurance are only useful when there are gains and significant accumulation of money.

Term insurance (temporary insurance) does not offer tax-free withdrawals and tax-deferred earnings because of the lack of cash build up. Minimum to no cash value build up in a permanent life policy will yield little to no tax advantages as well.

~ 31

Wake Up Action Step: You can only withdraw where you deposit. Study the amount of taxes that are paid. Use financial vehicles that can protect life and build cash value into the future.

Life of Annuity

February 1, 2023

An annuity is a long-term investment that's issued by an insurance company and is designed to help protect you from the risk of outliving your income. Through annuitization, your purchase payments (what you contribute) are converted into periodic payments that can last for a life.

People are becoming increasingly concerned about living a retirement life longer than what's initially planned for. An annuity is a savings version of a life insurance product. Annuities are either deferred or immediate. Structuring the correct annuity can pay out for a life span, so choose wisely.

~ 32 ~

Wake Up Action Step: Invest in a skillset that can pay you throughout your life. What skills do you naturally have? Write out every skill you believe you have and focus on the top two. Commit to one year of developing and mastering a skill. You owe you the highest form of yourself.

A Deferred Life of Annuity

February 2, 2023

Either invest in your life today or pay for it tomorrow. A deferred annuity is an insurance contract that generates income for retirement in exchange for one-time or recurring deposits held for at least a year.

An annuity company provides incremental repayments of your investment plus some amount of returns. Deferred annuities are taxed accounts where the owner invests in a 401(k) or IRA or makes consistent payments over a course of years. The consistent payments are referred to as the accumulation phase where cash grows and builds up.

~ 33

Wake Up Action Step: Do not wait to invest; invest and wait. Research about the accumulation phase today. Learn what kind of financial vehicle you're using for your retirement future. Start planning today!

An Immediate Life of Annuity

February 3, 2023

An immediate annuity is the most basic type of annuity and can create an immediate and guaranteed stream of income. You make one lump-sum contribution. That lump-sum is then converted into an ongoing, guaranteed stream of income for a specified period (as few as five years) or for a lifetime. Withdrawals may begin within a year.

~ 34

Wake Up Action Step: Leverage the power of an annuity by positioning your finances. Invest today, so you can harvest tomorrow and, in the days, months, and years to come.

Annuity Accumulation

February 4, 2023

Annuity accumulation is essential. Accumulation phase deals with deferred annuities. In the accumulation phase, contributions build up gradually and over time. Most annuities allow the holder of the policy to partially withdraw within their contract without penalty. Early withdrawals may incur a surrender charge. When withdrawing before the age of 59 and a half, there may be a 10 percent federal income tax penalty. Enhance your life by contributing and investing in skills that improve you as a person. Never stop accumulating!

~ 35 ~

Wake Up Action Step: Determine today that you'll start working towards your highest self. What areas in your life can you improve on? Do not sell yourself short by withdrawing a life you have not deposited in. Accumulate and grow annually.

Annuity Payout

February 5, 2023

Annuity payout is essential. Annuitization is known as the payout phase. Annuitization is the process of converting an annuity investment into a series of periodic income payments. Annuities may be annuitized for a specific period or for the life of the annuitant. Annuity payments may only be made to the annuitant or to the annuitant and a surviving spouse in a joint life arrangement. Pay out the cost today to build a life that will pay dividends through a lifetime. Move towards the direction of periodic and constant income of happiness, love, and peace.

~ 36 ~

Wake Up Action Step: Write out every major negative situation that has occurred in your life. List one way you can turn that negative situation into a positive one. Convert the pain of the past into the purpose of the present and future.

Annuity Period

February 6, 2023

Understanding period certain, is key to understanding how annuities work. Period certain is an annuity option that allows the customer to choose when and how long to receive payments, in which beneficiaries can later receive.

~ 37 ~

Wake Up Action Step: Choose you today. Every day you must decide to become the best version of yourself.

Will you choose your highest version? Be honest with yourself. Ultimately, actions are the biggest contributor to sustained success. Speak Life.

Annuity for a Lifetime and Period Certain

February 7, 2023

Combining annuity with period certain is a powerful retirement tool. A life annuity with period certain is a hybrid option that provides lifetime payments with guaranteed income for a specified number of years. Joint and survivor annuities are typically for those who are married. If one of the spouses dies, payment will continue onto the surviving spouse.

~ 38 ~

Wake Up Action Step: Secure your personal life. Start to position and protect your life and the life of your loved one. Live with purpose.

A Variable Life

February 8, 2023

Understanding the quality of life, you want to live is essential when planning for your future. The best way to determine the future is to plan it. Having the proper life insurance in place for yourself and your family is important when protecting key assets.

Variable life insurance is a permanent life insurance policy with an investment component. The policy has a cash-value account, which is invested in several other accounts that are available in the policy. A sub-account acts like a mutual fund, but only available within a variable life insurance policy. Cash-value in a variable life insurance policy can be accessed tax free when it's built up.

~ 39 ~

Wake Up Action Step: Take time to learn and master your ability to leverage assets. A variable life insurance policy contains cash-value that can be used and invested. Make sure you are properly protected and structured.

A Guaranteed Life

February 9, 2023

Investing in an annuity is a great way to use money. A joint and survivor annuity is a type of immediate annuity that guarantees payments for as long as the annuity owner or the beneficiary lives. The payments from a joint and survivor annuity would last the duration of the annuity owner's life plus the life of another person. Some may use the policy for or with a spouse. The payment continues to the spouse until his or her last day.

~ 40 ~

Wake Up Action Step: Make a list of expenses that must be paid within a lifetime. Properly plan and invest in the necessary financial vehicles. Live a life that guarantees abundance.

Annuities and Life Insurance

February 10, 2023

Annuities pay a set amount monthly, quarterly, or annually to meet financial needs in retirement. Life insurance is a little different in that it pays the value of the policy at death. For those who believe they may outlive their policy, an annuity may be a good option. Both life insurance and annuities offer different features. Choose the right product for you today.

~ 41 ~

Wake Up Action Step: Be proactive and use today to structure and expand your tomorrow.

Annuity Fixed

February 11, 2023

Annuities can be fixed. Fixed annuities are insurance products which protect against loss and generally offer fixed rates of return. The rates are typically based on the current interest rate environment. Fixed annuities guarantee a fixed rate of return. Returns are credited by a market index. The index normally has a minimum floor and a maximum cap.

There is no maximum contribution for annuities. One can invest as much as they'd like into the policy. Fix your goals on your highest and best self.

~ 42 ~

Wake Up Action Step: Fixed annuities have a lifetime payout. 401(k)s and IRAs are easily rolled over into the product. Capitalize on every opportunity. Use today to maximize everything!

Primary Markets

February 12, 2022

Primary markets are essential. When a company decides to raise money by offering its stock to investors, it'll sell the security in the primary market. The company sells stocks and bonds through an Initial Public Offering (IPO). The IPO is the first-time company certificates are being offered to the public. Understanding and leveraging primary markets correctly can create an extra stream of income that can replace a 9 to 5. Work smarter, not harder. The choice is yours.

~ 43 ~

Wake Up Action Step: Take 30 minutes today to research and study primary markets. Multiple streams of income await you.

Primary Markets: Part. 2

February 13, 2023

Primary markets control and dictate many areas of the economy. Many companies are large and successful when they go through the IPO process. To scale and grow their enterprise, large amounts of money typically are required to build new offices, purchase needed equipment, and hire the right staff. Capital is needed to expand, but a plan and a strategy to maximize markets is the most important. Plan and apply accordingly.

~ 44 ~

Wake Up Action Step: Create a plan of implementation today. Take inventory where you are currently. Study what you have. Utilize the resources you have, so you can get what and where you would like to be.

Primary Markets: Part. 3

February 14, 2023

Raising capital is one of the most important responsibilities for a company. When a company sells its stock in an IPO, it does so to raise money. The company is leveraging capital for capital – the ability to be liquid. Liquidity refers to the ease, in which an asset or security can be converted into ready cash without affecting its market price. Cash is the most liquid of assets.

~ 45 ~

Wake Up Action Step: Learn the art of personal liquidity. Liquify your personal skills and assets. The ability to monetize your gifts and talents will pay dividends for years to come.

Primary Markets: Part. 4

February 15, 2023

Primary distribution is the original sale of a security to the investing public. When stock is sold to the public for the first time, it could be considered a primary or secondary distribution. If a sale of securities occurs and the proceeds go to the issuer, it is considered a primary distribution.

~ 46 ~

Wake Up Action Step: Understand the right time to sell and hold. Each day, ask yourself, will selling this asset right now help or hurt me? Is selling my position the highest and best use of the asset? Start positioning today!

Secondary Markets

February 16, 2023

Secondary markets play a vital role in the economy. The secondary market is where investors buy and sell securities, in which they already own. It's what most people typically think of as the stock (market), which is sold on the primary market when initially offered. After an Initial Public Offering (IPO), investors can buy, sell, and trade certificates on the stock market.

~ 47 ~

Wake Up Action Step: Build where you are planted. Start from your initial position and leverage every opportunity to move to secondary and tertiary opportunities.

The Stock Market

February 17, 2023

The stock market is a platform of buyers and sellers of stocks. A stock market, equity market, or share market is the aggregation of buyers and sellers of stocks, which represent ownership claims on different businesses. Securities listed on a public stock exchange and privately traded stocks are also listed and traded. A stock is an instrument that signifies equity ownership in a corporation.

~ 48 ~

Wake Up Action Step: Sell or be sold. In most conversations surrounding the stock market, someone is either selling a concept and/or an idea or being sold. Take a position and commit to your share.

Bonds

February 18, 2023

Bonds play a vital role in the economy. A bond is a type of security under which the issuer owes the holder a debt and is obliged depending on the terms - to repay the principal of the bond at the maturity date as well as interest over a specified amount of time. Interest is usually payable at fixed intervals. Bonds are a good place to start to build capital for a company.

~ 49 ~

Wake Up Action Step: Build your capital today. Write out all the potential financial vehicles you can invest in. Begin today to build a life you don't need a vacation from.

The Market Index

February 19, 2023

The market index is a strong indicator of the current economy. A market index measures the value of a portfolio of holdings with specific market characteristics. Each index has its own methodology which is calculated and maintained by the index provider. Index methodologies will typically be weighted by either price or market cap. Market indexes also track the performance of a certain group of stocks, bonds, or other investments. The investments are often grouped around a particular industry.

~ 50 ~

Wake Up Action Step: Create and expand your market. Understand the value you bring to any and every market. Start today to perfect and fine tune your craft and skill set.

The Market Index: Part 2

February 20, 2023

The market index is a strong indicator of the current economy. There are different money market indexes such as the Dow Jones, S&P 500, and the NASDAQ. An index is a statistical indicator used to measure and report change in the market value of a group of stocks. The rise and fall of stocks are an indicator of index performance. Stocks and indexes do work together, but they are not the same.

~ 51 ~

Wake Up Action Step: Diversify your portfolio. Invest in different stocks. Do not hedge your investment into one stock. Take time to study the performance of those stocks. Double down on the best performing stocks. Begin your investing future today!

The Dow Index

February 21, 2023

The Dow Jones Industrial Average, Dow Jones, or simply the Dow is a price-weighted measurement stock market index of 30 prominent companies listed on the stock exchanges in the United States.

The Dow is the most well-known index in the world. The Dow Jones is also considered the barometer of the U.S. stock market. The Dow gives a good snapshot of how major corporations are performing nationwide but doesn't properly show how small to midsize companies are faring. Understand your market. Position yourself to be a leader in your market and industry.

~ 52 ~

Wake Up Action Step: Study your market. Understand what product or service you bring to the marketplace. Learn to dominate and excel in your field.

The S&P 500

February 22, 2023

The Standard and Poor's 500, or simply the S&P 500, is a stock market index that tracks the performance of 500 of the largest companies listed on the stock exchange. The S&P 500 is one of the most followed equity indexes.

The 500 comprises 70 percent of the U.S. economy. Some of the sectors included in the S&P 500 are real estate, hospitality, financials, health care, tech, retail, energy, and IT. The S&P 500 best reflects the U.S. economy and is used most frequently.

~ 53 ~

Wake Up Action Step: Increase your influence within your industry. The ability to influence and affect an industry can have a direct effect on the national economy. Either you'll be influenced by others, or you'll influence others. Stay the course and become and influencer today!

The NASDAQ

February 23, 2023

The Nasdaq is a global electronic marketplace for buying and selling securities. Its name was originally an acronym for 'National Association of Securities Dealers Automated Quotations.' The Nasdaq lists the stocks of over 3000 companies. The technology stocks include Tesla, Microsoft, Cisco, Intel, Apple, Netflix, and Amazon.

In other countries outside of the U.S., indexes track the stocks of large companies throughout the world. Indexes such as the Nikkei in Japan and Euro Stoxx in Europe are all located outside of The U.S. Globalization has made the world smaller and more connected. Understanding how you fit in a larger global economy can pay dividends for years to come.

~ 54 ~

Wake Up Action Step: Work to build a life that's impactful locally and internationally. Never limit yourself. Live and build globally today.

The Money Market

February 24, 2023

The money market is a component of the economy which provides short-term funds. The money market works with short-term loans, generally for a period of one year or less. Thus, is a market for low-risk securities. For example, bank certificates of deposit (CDs), commercial paper, and U.S. Treasury Bills are all low-risk securities.

Money market accounts are offered through credit unions and banks. Typically, these types of accounts yield higher returns than regular accounts but require higher deposits. Expand your market. Invest consistently and wisely.

~ 55 ~

Wake Up Action Step: Think long-term but invest in short-term increments. Start your financial game plan today. Time waits for no one.

The Mutual Fund

February 25, 2023

A mutual fund is a company that pools money from many investors and invests the money in securities such as stocks, bonds, and short-term debt. The total holdings of the mutual fund are known as a portfolio. Investors can buy shares in mutual funds. The popularity of mutual funds has increased throughout the years. When choosing the right mutual fund, focus on investments that can gain a rate of return higher than inflation.

~ 56 ~

Wake Up Action Step: Work and combine your natural resources. Mutual effort is more impactful and lasting. Work towards your strengths and downplay your weaknesses.

The Mutual Funds: Part: 2

February 26, 2023

The key to winning in the stock game is to spread out your risks. A mutual fund is a pool of money from investors. Each fund has a specific mandate or purpose and a professional fund manager who invests the money based on the specific strategy and goal of the fund. There are thousands of mutual funds options to choose from:

a. Balanced funds contain a mix of stocks and bonds.

b. Money market funds invest in highly liquid, near-term instruments. Some of the invested instruments include cash, cash equivalent securities, and U.S. treasuries.

c. Bond funds purchase primarily government and/or corporate bonds.

d. Stock funds are the most popular fund. Stock funds buy shares in companies typically traded on the stock exchange

~ 57 ~

Wake Up Action Step: Choosing the right mutual fund to invest in can be difficult, but not impossible. Before investing in any fund, take time to research the fund's financial plan. What's the expected return on investment? Ask yourself these questions and research the investment vehicle before investing a cent.

The Mutual Funds: Part: 3

February 27, 2023

Stocks remain popular, offering a wide range of funds. Stock funds are grouped into four main categories:

a. Index funds focus on achieving returns like a particular index such as the S&P 500

b. Growth funds focus mostly on capital appreciation, which is the increase in price or value of an asset. The appreciation of company stocks or bonds held by an investor, an increase in land valuation, or other upward revaluation of fixed assets.

c. Value funds focus more on stocks that are regarded as undervalued in price and likely to pay regular dividends

d. Sector funds focus on a particular industry segment such as biotech, energy, real estate, and emerging markets

~ 58 ~

Wake Up Action Step: Every mutual fund has their advantages and disadvantages. It's important to find a strategy and method that works best for you. Stick with the winning formula and double down in the areas that consistently produce, while eliminating the areas that do not. May the force be with you. Start working towards your investing future today!

The Mutual Funds: Part: 4

February 28, 2023

Every investment will incur some type of fee or expense. A mutual fund can carry a load or no load. A load is a mutual fund that comes with a sales charge or commission. The fund investor pays the load, which goes to compensate a sales intermediary, such as a broker, financial planner, or investment advisor. It's important to study a fund's simplified prospectus, which contains information about risks, fees, and charges.

Funds are required to disclose fees and charges per the Securities and Exchange Commission (SEC). Before investing in a particular fund, do your due diligence. The more work you do on the front end, the more you can benefit on the backend.

~ 59 ~

Wake Up Action Step: Use today to evaluate where you are financially. Never despise humble beginnings. Leverage your current position to empower yourself for today and tomorrow. Start to build now!

The Advantages of Mutual Funds

March 1, 2023

Mutual funds have key advantages that can create opportunities for the present and future. There are five key areas that are advantageous for mutual funds. See below.

a. Diversification: one of the best ways to lower risk is through diversification. Never put all your eggs into one basket. Spread capital across different bonds, stocks, and assets

b. Low investment minimums: the barrier of entry is relatively low. As low as $50.00 a month, one can begin investing

c. Professional management: wealth managers provide investment expertise in researching, monitoring, and selecting the performance of the securities purchases

d. Ease and convenience: it's relatively easy to set up pre-authorized checking programs for dollar cost averaging and ongoing purchases

e. Liquidity: it's easy to take your money out. You can take in and take out funds fluidly and quickly.

~ 60 ~

Wake Up Action Step: Understand the benefits of mutual funds. Nothing is truly guaranteed. Start today to utilize the benefits of assets.

The Disadvantages of Mutual Funds

March 2, 2023

High expense ratios and sales charges, management abuses, tax inefficiency, and poor trade execution are a few disadvantages of mutual funds. Ultimately, no one can truly guarantee monetary gains. Wealth managers are humans and can be wrong with their selections. The fees and expenses that are accumulated can reduce the overall profit of a fund.

~ 61 ~

Wake Up Action Step: Understand and manage risk. There is no investment that will not require some level of risk. Use today to study the risks associated with mutual funds. Take the necessary time to self-assess your personal skill set

Money Making with Mutual Funds

March 3, 2023

There are many ways you can start building wealth with mutual funds. The three main ways to create money with mutual funds include:

a. Returns on income. Mutual fund returns can yield profits from bond interest, stock dividends, and the selling of stock

b. Capital gains from distributions. When a stock is sold for more than what is initially invested, capital gains can be earned. The price of the securities a fund owns may increase when the fund sells them Appreciation of price. Investors can earn profits by selling their mutual fund units at a price that is higher than their initial investment

~ 62 ~

Wake Up Action Step: Create a life that's profitable. Work to make yourself an asset. Study and understand the demand and supply of the marketplace. Fine-tune your skill set to reflect what the market is demanding.

The Exchange Traded Fund

March 4, 2023

An exchange-traded fund (ETF) is a form of pooled investment security that operates like a mutual fund. ETFs follow a specific index, commodity, asset, or sector, but can be purchased or sold on an open stock market much like a stock. ETFs can be structured to track the price of an individual commodity to a large and diverse collection of securities. An ETF can also track specific investment strategies. Investing in an ETF can help protect and diversify an investment portfolio. Be invested, but never completely spent.

~ 63 ~

Wake Up Action Step: Study your market before investing. Understand what and why you are investing in the first place. If you're not investing and holding for at least 10 to 20 years, the risk of loss dramatically increases. Know and understand who you are as an investor.

A Variable Life

March 5, 2023

Understanding the quality of life, you want to live is essential when planning for your future. The best way to determine the future is to plan it. Having the proper life insurance in place for yourself and your family is important when protecting key assets.

Variable life insurance is a permanent life insurance policy with an investment component. The policy has a cash-value account, which is invested in several other accounts that are available in the policy. A sub-account acts like a mutual fund, but only available within a variable life insurance policy. Cash-value in a variable life insurance policy can be accessed tax free when it's built up.

~ 64 ~

Wake Up Action Step: Take time to learn and master your ability to leverage assets. A variable life insurance policy contains cash-value that can be used and invested. Make sure you are properly protected and structured.

A Variable Life: Part 2

March 5, 2023

The ability to build capital is one of the unique features of a variable life policy. The cash value account has the potential to grow as the underlying investments in the policy's sub-accounts grow. As the underlying drops, so may the cash value.

Variable life insurance is an insurance policy, in which the payouts are determined by the performance of the underlying securities in the policy. Variable life insurance policies are considered more volatile than standard life insurance policies and are ideal only for those individuals that understand the risk. Variable life return can be inconsistent and moving but can yield higher and stronger profits over a period.

~ 65 ~

Wake Up Action Step: Variable life gains and growth are exponential, but the lose can also be rapid. Where you can gain on the growth, you can also lose on the losses. Build a strong profile by investing in varied asset classes. Start investing as soon as possible. Time is the greatest factor in most to all investments.

A Variable Life: Part 3

March 5, 2023

Another major advantage of a variable life policy is the tax advantages. Variable policies have tax advantages whether the policy preforms well or not. The main draw of variable life insurance is the investment aspect coupled with favorable tax treatment. Growth of the cash value within the policy is not taxed as ordinary or w2 income. Cash value in these policies can be drawn on after a few years of cash build up.

You can leverage a loan and use the actual policy as collateral. Instead of direct withdrawals, funds may be received free of income tax. As with any investment, there will be fees and expenses that are assessed with each asset.

~ 66 ~

Wake Up Action Step: Learning the tax code of any country will reveal what's important to the governing body currently in place. Start today to understand how the tax law is written. Variable life has several tax advantages many other financial vehicles don't have. Variable life insurance is incentivized for a reason. Take advantage today!

The Variable Annuity

March 5, 2023

A variable annuity is a type of annuity contract. The value of the contact is based on the performance of an underlying portfolio of sub-accounts. When investing in a fixed annuity, the insurance company yields a fixed rate of return. The policy owner is responsible to choose the different investment options with variable annuities.

The main purpose of annuities for most people is to plan for their long-term retirement. It's essential to understand the risks of any investment portfolio. Variable annuity account values will fluctuate with market conditions, and once redeemed, may be less valuable than the original value.

~ 67 ~

Wake Up Action Step: Start planning today for tomorrow. Long-term investment and payoff can't be created or sustained in one day. You must be intentional when planning for a life of retirement. Start now!

The Variable Annuity: Part 2

March 6, 2023

The value of variable annuity is based on the performance of the policy. Variable annuities offer the possibility of higher returns and greater income than fixed annuities, but there's also a risk the account will fall in value. There are two elements that contribute to the value of a variable annuity: the principal, which is the amount of money paid into the annuity, and the annuity's investment that's paid out over the course of time.

The most popular type of variable annuity is a deferred annuity. Deferred annuities are often used for retirement planning purposes. This type of annuity is meant to provide a stream of income monthly, quarterly, and annually.

~ 68 ~

Wake Up Action Step: Determine today what's more important when planning for a solid financial future. Decide what kind of investor you want to become. The journey of a million miles started with a single step, so take the necessary steps today.

The Variable Annuity: Part 3

March 7, 2023

You can purchase an annuity with either a lump sum or series of payments. The account's value will grow accordingly. Deferred annuities are often referred to as the accumulation phase. The second phase is triggered when the annuity owner asks the insurer to start the flow of income, often referred to as the payout phase.

Most annuities won't allow withdrawal of additional funds from the account once the payout phase has begun. Variable annuities should be considered a long-term investment. Invest wisely.

~ 69 ~

Wake Up Action Step: Take the time to study and learn the best time to withdraw funds from a well-funded account. Practice and plan your way forward. Write out the pros and cons of a variable annuity. Start building today!

The Variable Annuity: Part 4

March 8, 2023

Variable annuities have limitations on withdrawals and is considered a long-term investment. Generally, only one withdrawal is allowed per year during the accumulation phase. A surrender fee will be assessed for any withdrawals done during the surrender period.

Variable annuities were introduced in the 1950s. Variable annuities were looked at as an alternative to fixed annuities and gave buyers a chance to benefit from rising markets by investing in a mutual fund. Buyers earn higher returns but are left exposed to market risk and loss. For instance, there's a 10 percent tax penalty for withdrawals made before age 59 ½.

~ 70 ~

Wake Up Action Step: Structure the right investments at the right time. Understand the right time to make withdrawals. Investing at the wrong time can waste energy, resources, and opportunities. Take your time and invest well today.

Variable Annuities Advantages

March 9, 2023

Variable annuities have a tax-deferred growth. Taxes on the product are not taxed until you begin receiving income or make a withdrawal. Income stream can be suited for your needs. Funds in an annuity are protected against creditors and other debt collectors. There are many advantages of variable annuities. The correct policy can pay a lifetime of benefits.

~ 71 ~

Wake Up Action Step: If you're not enlightened or educated in a particular area, it's your responsibility to take the time to educate yourself. Make the money, grow the money, and maximize any and every asset.

Time Above All

March 10, 2023

Time is the most important asset. Understanding how to leverage time properly can open many opportunities. Identifying your objective and outlining your goals is a first step in getting those opportunities. With these key areas, you can select the right tools or investment(s) for a project or task. The two biggest factors in determining the right investment(s) are risk tolerance and time. Knowing when and where to invest will also influence your investment strategy.

~ 72 ~

Wake Up Action Step: Start building today. The number of years an investment is expected to be in the market affects the rate of return. If you're expecting a turnaround of capital within a year timeframe, you may want to remain liquid throughout.

Variable Annuities Disadvantages

March 11, 2023

Variable annuities pose more risk than fixed annuities because the investment can potentially lose value. There are surrender fees applied to certain type of withdrawals. Any withdrawals made prior to the age of 59 ½, will have a 10 percent tax penalty. Variable typically carry more fees.

Before investing in variable annuity, take the time to read the prospectus. It's important to understand the expenses and risks associated with investing in variable annuities.

~ 73

Wake Up Action Step: Rewards and risks go hand and hand. Reward is not possible without risk. Change the way you view risks. Calculated risks are necessary for progress and advancement. Ultimately, taking no risks at all may be the riskiest position. Start today to take practical steps towards your future with well thought out, planned risks and rewards.

Learn to invest

March 12, 2023

The ability to properly invest can open opportunities for generations to come. Investing early can pay huge dividends but remaining positive is key when investing. Past performance is not an indication of future results, but understanding the numbers is important.

When investing know and understand that the data, statistics, rates of return, and dividend yields are based on the past and prior performance is not equivalent to future gains and results. It's truly impossible to guarantee future performance, so maintain the correct perspective no matter the situation. Data and information are all relative. Leverage the technology and stats accordingly. Today is a brand-new day, so move with confidence.

~ 74 ~

Wake Up Action Step: Past performance is not an automatic indicator of future results. Take time to understand the market and industry of choice. Plan a course of action and work to execute your plan. With each rep, repeat the process and add momentum with confidence. Remember, learners are earners. Learn and earn more today!

Time is the Greatest Asset

March 13, 2023

Ultimately, time cannot be owned by any one person. Time can be managed and leveraged if used properly. The greatest factor in any investment is the time factor. Understanding your personal goals and objectives can dramatically improve potential investments and opportunity. Risk tolerance and time can play an important role when selecting what to invest in. If one plans to have their money invested for less than a year, it will be wise to keep the funds inside of a savings account or in a money market account. Liquidity is a company's ability to raise cash when needed.

~ 75 ~

Wake Up Action Step: There are two major determinants of a company's liquidity position. The first is the ability to turn an asset to cash to pay its current or past liabilities. The second is its debt capacity. Debt capacity refers to the total amount of debt a business can incur and repay according to the terms of a debt agreement.

Time Is the Greatest Asset: Part 2

March 14, 2023

Time is to be utilized and managed. Understanding how time should be used and leveraged can open a lifetime of opportunities. If you're looking to be invested within one to five years, consider safe vehicles like CD's, GICs, and Treasury Bills. The longer an investment, the larger the return.

For investments five years or longer, consider stocks, bonds, or real estate. The longer you invest the money, the greater chance you have to increase the amount of stock in your investment portfolio. Statistics show that investors who keep their investment in stocks for 20 years typically don't suffer losses.

~ 76 ~

Wake Up Action Step: Past performance does not automatically guarantee future results. Time in the market is more important than trying to time the market. If you don't invest, you'll dramatically decrease your opportunity at financial freedom and generational wealth. Start today to build the future you can be proud of and enjoy!

Allocate Assets

March 15, 2023

Save to invest; don't invest just to save. Spread your risk out and never invest 100 percent into one financial vehicle. Diversification over time will consistently yield the highest return. Study the performance of each asset class. Double down on the top performing investments.

Conservative investors who invest at least 35 percent of their fixed income, tend to have the lowest returns; moderate investors who invest at least 50 percent of their fixed income tend to have the second lowest returns; moderately aggressive investors who invest at least 70 percent of their income tend to have the second most returns. Aggressive investors are those who invest 90 percent of their earned income.

~ 77 ~

Wake Up Action Step: Invest constantly, freely, and sooner than later. By investing well and constantly over an extended period will guarantee success. Do not underestimate the power of repetition. Persistence will always counter resistance. Follow a plan for investing and stick to what works. May the odds and probability be with you.

Cost Averaging of the Dollar

March 16, 2023

Dollar cost averaging is the practice of investing a fixed dollar amount on a regular basis, regardless of the share price. Dollar cost averaging is a good way to develop a disciplined investing habit, while becoming more efficient in how you invest.

By mitigating the risk of loss, an investor can invest with less stress and focus. The strategy systematically purchases shares of security products to offset investment risk in a fluctuating market.

~ 78 ~

Wake Up Action Step: Dollar cost averaging helps one to continue investing the same dollar amount every month buying into the same amount shares. If the share price goes up, you buy fewer shares. If the share price goes down, you buy more shares. Invest now, often, and freely.

Actual Rate of Return

March 17, 2023

Understanding the actual rate of return can pay dividends in the short and long term. Let's say you invest $100.00, and you had a 50 percent loss the first year, and in the second year a 50 percent gain. What would you predict was the overall rate of return? Would you predict the overall rate return zeroed out? After the first year of investing $100.00 with a 50 percent loss, the overall earning after year one was $50.00. The second year yielded a 50 percent profit, but the 50 percent increase was from the $50.00 which would be an overall return of $75.00. This means that after two years of being completely invested, the overall return was a 25 percent loss.

~ 79 ~

Wake Up Action Step: The actual rate of return can be deceptive. Use today to study the actual return of investments over time. As an investor, don't assume the average rate of return is enough. Ultimately, numbers speak a language, and only the effective translation of those numbers can serve us. Start building today!

Actual Rate of Return: Part 2

March 18, 2023

The actual rate of return was much greater than the average rate of return. Unfortunately, this is the reason many people, especially in the U.S. retire broke.

After the housing bubble burst and the dot.com era, the market fell by more than 45 percent in 2000 and by over 50 percent in 2008. By the time the market finally bounced back, it was already too late for many retirees. Many retirement plans and lives were destroyed forever. Proper management requires an attention to detail.

~ 80 ~

Wake Up Action Step: Financial illiteracy has robbed more lives than any other ideology or concept ever created. Take time to address the misconceived notions and mindsets. Build a proper mindset every day and take life one day at a time. Be honest and realistic about what you don't know and understand. What you don't know could hurt you in the long run.

Strategy over Emotions

March 19, 2023

Money has no soul or emotion. Money follows strategic and efficient management. You may not know how the stock market will perform each day, but one thing that's been proven is that the stock market has historically moved up over an extended period of time. Emotionally investing may leave you frustrated, tired and at a loss.

Some investors want to know the short-term ups and downs and disregard long-term growth and potential. Entering the market at the wrong time can have a negative impact on return. Selling stocks too early can also contribute to losses.

~ 81 ~

Wake Up Action Step: Consistency combined with time is the greatest indicator of success in the stock market. Being overly emotional when investing is almost a sure way to be unsuccessful in the investing world. Invest well and invest often.

Defined Benefit Plan

March 20, 2023

A defined benefit plan is an employer sponsored retirement plan where employee benefits are computed using a formula that considers several factors, such as length of employment and salary history. The company is responsible for managing the plan's investments and risks, and usually hires an outside investment manager to do the work. A defined benefit plan is also known as a traditional pension. A retiree is paid a specific benefit based on years of service and salary until death. In some cases, the payout will continue for a spouse or a beneficiary.

~ 82 ~

Wake Up Action Step: Defined benefit plan is costly for the employer. The reality is that these kinds of plans are being phased out. No matter the age, start building income streams today. Even if one plans to work for their entire life, it is important to plan and work towards a life of multiple streams of income.

Defined Benefit Plan: Part 2

March 21, 2023

Typically, an employee cannot withdraw funds from their defined benefit plan in the same way as with a 401(k) plan. Instead, they become eligible to take their benefit as a lifetime annuity, or in some cases as a lump sum at an age defined by the plan's rules.

Funds from a defined benefit plan are different from other retirement funds. Payouts are not dependent on investment returns. Poor investment returns or faulty assumptions and calculations can result in a funding shortfall. Employers are legally obligated to make up the difference with a cash contribution.

~ 83 ~

Wake Up Action Step: Benefits can be distributed as fixed monthly payments like an annuity or in one lump-sum payment. The surviving spouse is often entitled to the benefits if the employee passes away. The employer assumes all the investment and planning risks. Work and build for the life that you desire. A world full of opportunity is in front of you.

Defined Contribution Plan

March 22, 2023

A defined contribution (DC) plan is a retirement plan that's typically tax-deferred, like a 401(k) or a 403(b), in which employees contribute a fixed amount or a percentage of their paychecks to an account intended to fund their retirement. The sponsor company will match a portion of employee contributions as an added benefit. Defined contribution plans have restrictions that control when and how each employee can withdraw from these accounts without penalties.

~ 84 ~

Wake Up Action Step: The earlier you start investing into your defined contribution plan, the more opportunity there is to grow your retirement. Build and invest into your plan today. The way to determine the future is to plan and work towards the future you desire. The world is yours.

Defined Contribution Plan: Part. 2

March 23, 2023

Defined contribution (DC) retirement plans allow employees to invest pre-tax dollars in the capital markets where they can grow tax-deferred until retirement. This allows the account to grow at a faster rate without the burden of taxes.

Two popular DC plans include 401(k) and 403(b). These two plans are commonly used by companies and organizations to encourage their employees to save for retirement. Defined contribution plans can be contrasted with defined benefit (DB) pensions, in which retirement income is guaranteed by an employer.

~ 85 ~

Wake Up Action Step: There are no guarantees, and participation is voluntary and self-directed with a DC plan. Take time to research the different retirement options your company may offer. Having an employer willing to match contributions can help create a retirement account that may grow to a significant amount.

Defined Contribution Plan: Part.

March 24, 2023

Your employer serves as the sponsor of the plan. The plan administrator is typically a mutual fund company, a brokerage firm, or an insurance company. You are responsible for the investment of your money by choosing investment options within the plan.

A 401(k) is a retirement savings account which offers tax advantages. This plan is an employer-sponsored, defined-contribution, personal pension account, as defined in subsection 401(k) of the U.S. Internal Revenue Code. Periodical employee contributions come directly out of their paychecks and may be matched by the employer.

~ 86 ~

Wake Up Action Step: Planning for retirement early on is a good decision. Building out a 401(k) account allows an individual and employer to contribute to an investment account that has certain tax advantages such as deferred taxes. Start today to build the future you deserve.

Defined Contribution Plan: Part. 4

March 25, 2023

A 403(b) plan is a U.S. tax-advantaged retirement savings plan available for public education organizations, some non-profit employers, cooperative hospital service organizations, and self-employed ministers. The 403(b) plan focuses on nonprofits and certain government agencies like public schools. The 403(b) plan has some disadvantages. For instance, access to withdrawals is typically restricted until age 59 ½, except under certain limited circumstances.

~ 87 ~

Wake Up Action Step: Early withdrawals are assessed a tax penalty of 10 percent. Withdrawals are taxed as income, not as capital gains. Patience is a virtue. Learn the art of delayed gratification. Patience pays and progresses.

Defined Contribution Plan: Part. 5

March 26, 2023

A 457 plan allows one to save and invest money for retirement with tax benefits. Assets in a 457 deferred compensation plan typically become available for withdrawal once an employee leaves employment. A 457 plan is a tax-deferred retirement savings plan. Savings can be withdrawn from an employee's income without being taxed and are only taxed upon withdrawal, which is typically at retirement, after the funds have had several years to grow. Employees make contributions as part of their paycheck, and if the employer offers a company match, the employer will make contributions as well.

~ 88 ~

Wake Up Action Step: Contributions are made to an account in the employee's name for the exclusive benefit of the employee and their beneficiaries. The account's value is based on the contributions made and the investment performance over time. Contribute and invest towards the life you want to live. Value increases with time, so use your time wisely.

Defined Contribution Plan: Part. 6

March 27, 2023

Defined contribution plans invest with pre-tax contributions. Withdrawing money before the age of 59 ½ will activate an early withdrawal penalty, but with a few exceptions. All distributions will be taxed as ordinary income. Defined contribution plans allow investors to know what has been contributed. The final return will be based on the fluctuations of the market. There are many areas of life that are not guaranteed, but there are two things that are: taxes and death.

~ 89 ~

Wake Up Action Step: Not planning is planning to fail. Take 10 minutes today to write out the type of life you're interested in living. Calculate your monthly income and set that number aside. Once you find a way to meet your monthly expenses, you're well on your way.

Passive Employees

March 28, 2023

The 401(k) plan and other defined contribution plans are popular, but many employees do not understand or properly utilize financial tools and resources.

Unfortunately, many employees are passive participants and only contribute to their retirement plans because they see others investing. A limited number of workers participate long-term, and an even lower percentage of employees understand and monitor their plan. Over 70 percent of people with 401(k)s did not know they were paying fees for their retirement account. Fees can reduce a 401(k) balance by over 28 percent.

~ 90 ~

Wake Up Action Step: Financial illiteracy has destroyed more lives than any one disease. Financial ignorance causes more stress in homes, marriages, and relationships than any other factor known to men. Without understanding the different investment options of the plan, one may pick an option that doesn't meet the risk tolerance or objective of the client. Failing to plan is planning to fail. Start planning well today.

Individual Retirement Account (IRA)

March 29, 2023

An Individual Retirement Account (IRA) is the most common retirement. An IRA allows you to save money for retirement in a tax-advantages way. An IRA is an account set up at a financial institution that allows an individual to save for retirement with tax-free growth or on a tax-deferred basis. One benefit of an IRA is that taxes are not paid on the money you contribute until it is withdrawn. Interest, dividends, and capital gains in the plan are all tax-deferred until withdrawal.

~ 91 ~

Wake Up Action Step: Plan for the life you desire. Unfortunately, many employees will retire with less than they expect and need. Utilize what's available. Invest in a savings and retirement account. An individual retirement account was created for the retirement life. Start planning today and work towards securing your tomorrow.

Roth Individual Retirement Account (IRA)

March 30, 2023

A Roth IRA is a type of tax-advantaged individual account to which one can contribute after-tax dollars. The advantage of a Roth IRA is that contributions and earnings can grow tax-free, and withdrawals are tax-free after the age of 59 ½, assuming the account has been open for at least five years. Traditional IRAs are like Roth IRAs. The major difference is how each account is taxed. Roth IRAs are funded with after-tax dollars, meaning the contributions are not tax-deductible. The withdrawn money is tax free.

~ *92* ~

Wake Up Action Step: Retirement is a reality that many people will face. By positioning assets and capital in the proper vehicles, retirement can be an enjoyable and prosperous time. Start today to find out which retirement vehicle will best position you for success.

Roth Individual Retirement Account (IRA): Part. 2

March 31, 2023

A Roth IRA is a special retirement account where you pay taxes on money going into your account, and then all future withdrawals are tax free. Roth IRAs are best when marginal taxes will be higher in retirement than they are right now.

Single filers cannot contribute to a Roth IRA if they earned more than $140,000.00 in 2021 and $144,000.00 in 2022. For married couples filing jointly, the limit was $208,000.00 in 2021, and $214,000.00 in 2022. The deductible amount that can be contributed changes annually. In 2021 and 2022, the contribution limit is $6,000.00 a year unless you are age 50 or older. Individuals 50 years old or older can deposit up to $7,000.00

~ 93 ~

Wake Up Action Step: Time does not wait. Time only moves in one direction, and that's forward. Focus on maximizing the current time you are in. Even if your income is not where you'd like, ask yourself, am I maximizing the resources I currently have? The answer to this question will determine the different future opportunities. Invest and maximize today.

Roth Individual Retirement Account (IRA): Part. 3

April 1, 2023

There are specific allowable investments in a Roth IRA. Once funds are contributed, a variety of investment options exist within a Roth IRA, including mutual funds, stocks, bonds, exchange-traded funds (ETFs), certificates of deposit (CDs), and now even cryptocurrency. Anyone who has earned income can contribute to a Roth IRA if they meet certain requirements concerning filing status and modifies adjusted gross income (MAGI).

~ 94 ~

Wake Up Action Step: Learning how taxes work in a particular country can pay dividends. The government will show you what areas are more valuable versus others based on how it's incentivized and taxed. Typically, areas that are incentivized and taxed less are encouraged by the government. Leverage tax law to benefit how you structure and operate your life.

The Five-Year Rule

April 2, 2023

Withdrawal of earnings may be subject to taxes and/or a 10 percent penalty, depending on your age and whether you have met the five-year rule. Earnings from individuals under age 59 ½ are subject to taxes and penalties. Individuals may be able to avoid taxes and penalties if the money withdrawn is used for a first-time home purchase. There is a $10,000.00 lifetime limit. If one has a permanent disability, or if they pass away, a beneficiary takes the distribution. Individuals aged 59 ½ and older avoid taxes and penalties.

~ 95 ~

Wake Up Action Step: Take time to learn and leverage the timing of life. There's a window of time for every opportunity and investment. Do not allow the deception of time to trick you into the belief of unlimited time. Time is a finite commodity, so use it wisely. Utilize and maximize the time you have left. Best of luck and may the force be with you!

IRA Rollovers

April 3, 2023

An IRA Rollover is an account that allows you to move funds from prior employer-sponsored retirement plans into an IRA. With an IRA rollover, you can preserve the tax-deferred status of retirement assets without paying current taxes or early withdrawal penalties. IRA rollovers are an important feature to move money to a better investment account. IRA rollovers can rollover one IRA into another. An IRA can be rolled into 401(k)s, 403(b)s, another IRA, and a Roth IRA.

~ 96 ~

Wake Up Action Step: Many people don't use their IRAs properly. Unfortunately, a large portion of capital will be left on the table. Many hardworking individuals leave billions on the table and leave unclaimed capital to their companies and the internal revenue service. Claim what's yours today. Invest today to find what's not being claimed and is owed to you.

Simple IRA

April 4, 2023

A Simple IRA, also known as a Savings Incentive Match Plan for Employees is ideal for small business owners because it lacks the reporting requirements and paperwork required for many other types of workplace retirement plans.

Both the employee and employer can contribute money to a Simple IRA. Employees can choose whether they want to contribute. Employers must make contributions. Employees may choose to save pre-tax income in their accounts, which provides the benefit of lowering overall taxable income. Employers make either dollar-for-dollar matching contributions equal to 1 to 3 percent of their employees' salary, or non-elective contributions equal to 2 percent of their salary. This happens regardless of whether a worker contributes.

~ *97* ~

Wake Up Action Step: Money saved in a Simple IRA can be invested in different securities and funds. Money located in Simple IRAs are tax-deferred. Taxes won't need to be paid on capital gains taxes. Taxes will be the largest expense for most adults. Take advantage of tax savings accounts today. Invest well and invest early!

SEP IRA

April 5, 2023

A simplified employee pension (SEP) is an individual retirement account (IRA) an employer or a self-employed person can establish. The employer is allowed a tax deduction for contributions made to a SEP IRA and makes contributions to each eligible employee's plan on a discretionary basis.

Employees do not pay taxes until withdrawals. Like other IRA plans, 59 ½ and 70 ½ rules apply. Withdrawals prior to age 59 ½ will receive a penalty with certain exceptions, such as medical or education expenses, or first-time home purchasing. Both SIMPLE and SEP IRAs are relatively simple and low cost to set up.

~ 98 ~

Wake Up Action Step: Start to plan for retirement as soon as possible. Take time to study and learn all the different investment vehicles that are available. Never assume what can be researched for accuracy. Plan, build, and execute the life you and your loved ones deserve.

Saving and Planning for College

April 6, 2023

Properly saving and planning for college can be a challenge, but with proper planning and execution, success is inevitable. It can cost a middle-income family up to $250,000.00 to raise a child for 18 years.

This cost does not include college tuition. Tuition for a private education can cost as much as $130,000.00 for a four-year degree and a public education can cost up to $40,000.00. Many parents prepare for everything except the cost of a quality education. Think ahead of the current times. Cut down on unnecessary spending, so you can increase your savings. Start investing early.

~ 99 ~

Wake Up Action Step: Look at opening a life insurance policy for a child when they're young. The younger the insured, the cheaper the policy. By starting early to open a policy, you can leverage the cash value to help cover the increasing tuition costs. Start today to think of creative ways to fund and finance your kids' future!

A 529 Savings Plan

April 7, 2023

A 529 plan is a tax-advantaged savings plan designed to encourage saving for future education costs. A 529 plan is legally known as a "qualified tuition plan," and are sponsored by states, state agencies, or educational institutions. They are authorized by Section 529 of the Internal Revenue Code.

Two types of 529 plans include prepaid tuition plans and education savings plans. Most states sponsor at least one type of 529 plan. A group of private colleges and universities also sponsor prepaid tuition plans.

~ 100 ~

Wake Up Action Step: Research the past, current, and future education costs. Contact the schools you plan for your child to attend. Figure out how much the institution is willing to sponsor. Set realistic financial goals that can be met and delivered. Save, invest, and progress.

A 529 Savings Plan: Part 2

April 8, 2023

With a 529 savings plan, parents can open an account and choose an investment strategy - money put in after taxes. Potential earnings accumulate tax free, and withdrawals can be made tax free when it's time to pay for college expenses, such as tuition, books, and room and board. Even though a 529 is state sponsored, it's still open to non-residents.

Parents can shop around for the plan that meets their financial goals and needs. If a child decides not to go to college, it's possible to transfer the money to another family member for college. If no one decides college is for them, then the money accumulated will be subject to regular income taxes plus a 10 percent penalty on gains.

~ 101 ~

Wake Up Action Step: At some point a child will grow to make their own decisions. Planning for their college fund is great, but ultimately some kids may decide not to further their education. However, don't let this stop you from planning accordingly. It's better to have something that's not needed, than to need something you don't have. Control what you can and release the rest. Remain encouraged and blessed.

A 529 Savings Plan: Part 3

April 9, 2023

Prepaid tuition plans allow the saver or account holder to purchase units or credits at participating colleges and universities for future tuition and mandatory fees at current prices for the beneficiary. If prepaid tuition payments aren't guaranteed, one may lose some or all their money in the plan if the plan's sponsor has a financial shortfall. If a beneficiary doesn't attend a participating college or university, the prepaid tuition plan may pay less. Education savings plans allow a saver to open an investment account to save for the beneficiary's future qualified higher expenses, like tuition, mandatory fees, and room and board.

~ 102 ~

Wake Up Action Step: Withdrawals from education savings plan accounts can generally, be used at any college or university, including sometimes at non-U.S. colleges and universities. Education savings plans can also be used to pay up to $10,000.00 per year per beneficiary for tuition at any public or private school. An investment in a good and sound education can pay back in many ways. Save and invest into education. Become a lifelong learner.

Registered Retirement Savings Plan

April 10, 2023

A Registered Retirement Savings Plan (RRSP) is a retirement savings and investing vehicle for employees and the self-employed. Pre-tax money is placed into an RRSP and grows tax-free until withdrawal, at which time it's taxed at the marginal rate. RRSPs have many features in common with 401(k) plans in the U.S., but also some key differences. The growth of a RRSP is determined by its contents and have two main tax advantages. First, contributors may deduct contributions against their income. Secondly, the growth of RRSP investments is tax-deferred. Unlike with non-RRSP investments, returns are exempt from any capital gains tax, dividend tax, or income tax.

~ 103 ~

Wake Up Action Step: Investments under RRSPs compound on a pre-deferred basis. All the growth inside RRSPs grows tax deferred until withdrawal. This can have a positive effect on the value of the RRSP since no tax is paid on any growth along the way. Taxes will be paid later when withdrawn. Taxes are a huge expense that must be planned for. Start today to learn how taxes work to leverage savings into increased income and revenue.

Registered Retirement Savings Plan

April 11, 2023

Registered Retirement Savings Plan (RRSP) contributors delay the payment of taxes until retirement when their marginal tax rate may be lower than during their working years. There are two main types of RRSPs. First, there's an individual RRSP set up by a single person who's both the account holder, and the contributor. Secondly, a spousal RRSP provides benefits for a single spouse and a tax benefit for both spouses. A high earner may contribute to a spousal RRSP in their spouse's name. Retirement income is divided evenly, and each spouse can benefit from a lower marginal tax rate.

~ 104 ~

Wake Up Action Step: Always work to build wealth. If you're focused on growing and expanding opportunities and capital, saving for retirement is much more manageable and doable.

Tax Free Savings Account

April 12, 2023

A tax-free savings account is a savings vehicle for saving inside a personal tax shelter. Always have different investment options. The benefits of a tax-free savings account are that no matter how much growth is inside an account, taxes won't have to be paid on it. When structuring a financial plan, utilize a tax-free savings account. Keep track of where capital is being invested. Never assume when investing. Take the time to learn an industry before investing.

~ 105 ~

Wake Up Action Step: Learn how investing works by reading about investments that have cash flow. Understanding cash flow while leveraging tax advantage accounts can serve as a powerful resource and tool.

Social Security

April 13, 2023

Social Security is a term used for the Old-Age, Survivors and Disability Insurance (OASDI). This is a program ran by the Social Security Administration (SSA), a federal agency. Social Security is best known for retirement benefits. It also provides survivor benefits and income for workers who become disabled. Social Security is a federal program that provides retirement benefits and disability income to qualified people and their spouses, children, and survivors. Social Security is funded by current payroll taxes (FICA) from an individual to an employer. Currently, there is a shrinking pool of workers per retiree.

~ 106 ~

Wake Up Action Step: Congress established the Social Security Act of 1935 to help supplement the incomes of retirees. Unfortunately, Social Security has become the only source of income for millions of Americans. It is grossly irresponsible to believe the government will save anyone. A properly structured plan is needed when planning for retirement and beyond.

Taxes on Your Social Security Benefit

April 14, 2023

Social Security is taxed depending on streams income. For example, salary from working, is taxed. Earning interest and capital gains is taxed. Withdrawals from retirement savings in an IRA, 403(b), 401(k), and earning gains from annuities distributions are all taxed.

Roth IRA distributions are income-tax free. There are a few financial vehicles that are tax free. Withdrawals and loans from insurance policies are not deemed a taxable event. Income from a married spouse is also taxed together. If one fails to make Required Minimum Distributions (RMD) at age 70 ½, there will be a 50 percent tax penalty on top of income tax on the RMD amount.

~ 107 ~

Wake Up Action Step: There are two things guaranteed to happen at some point: taxes will be paid on your behalf and death will occur. Knowing death and taxes are inevitable allows people the opportunity to properly plan and prepare for what's ahead.

Growth and Development

April 15, 2023

Growth is defined as an irreversible constant increase in size and development. Economic growth can be defined as the increase or improvement in the inflation-adjusted market value of the goods and services produced by an economy over a certain period. Growth can be measured as the percent rate of increase in the Real Gross Domestic Product (GDP). Many people are losing the money game. There are millions drowning in a sea of debt. Bankruptcies do not just happen to the working poor. It happens to people from all walks of life.

~ 108 ~

Wake Up Action Step: Some individuals make a lot, but they spend a lot too. Others make big bets when the market is hot, but shy away when the market is undervalued. Some lose and don't know why they lose. Those who win don't often know why they win. Information is the new currency. Most to all will adjust and change if they have the right information. Ignorance on how money works is one of the main causes of poverty and money issues.

Growth vs. Safety

April 16, 2023

You must choose which one is more important, growth or safety. When people think of the safety of their money, they tend to think of banks or savings. However, others may think of growth as investments and securities. If one desires true growth, they must be willing to understand the idea of safety as it pertains to investing.

If a rate of return is not growing faster than inflation, there's money being lost. The riskiest position to take is taking no risk at all. Mediocrity is the biggest threat to prosperity and wealth. Playing it safe can lead to an impoverished and subpar life.

~ 109 ~

Wake Up Action Step: Get in the game and take calculated chances. Constructive criticism constructs accomplishments. Success in life is like sports – you must play both offense and defense to win and thrive. Success requires defense and offense to be played simultaneously. It's important to be efficient on both ends. Diversify and allocate assets with confidence today.

Growth vs. Safety: Part 2

April 17, 2023

True growth requires confidence and courage. Growth, safety, tax advantage, and protection are all areas that can affect one's quality of life. Use dollar cost averaging to capitalize on the downtime in the market. As time changes, rebalance investments and restructure strategies that work and are effective.

When building towards a strong and solid future, you must ask yourself whether the potential growth can be achieved within a certain timeframe. Is the investment safe enough? Does the investment have tax advantages, and does it have proper protection? One is only able to grow as far as they can manage. Good management produces more opportunity and growth over an extended period of time.

$$\sim 110 \sim$$

Wake Up Action Step: It's not about how much you make; it's about how much you manage to keep. Maximize every blessing. How you manage your gifts may determine how much access and opportunities you'll receive in the present and the future. If you want more of anything in life, manage what you have better and more effectively. Start today to manage better and more effectively.

A 10/20 Plan

April 18, 2023

Many Americans need to save more. To retire comfortably it's advised to save at least 20 times your annual income. For family protection, it's advised to save at least 10 times of your annual income. An insurance policy can be used to accomplish this goal. By saving 10 times your annual income, family members have 10 years or more to prepare and adjust. You will need 10 times annual income to cover life insurance. People are now living longer, and more resources are needed to comfortably retire.

~ 111 ~

Wake Up Action Step: No one can plan and prepare for you. If you don't do the necessary work at the appropriate time, the only person to truly blame is yourself. The sad part of not planning is that by the time the individual finally realizes their life has literally become a burden and liabilities for their loved ones, it may be too late. Do yourself a favor and start now to plan and prepare. Tomorrow, you will thank you for it!

Medicare and Health Insurance

April 19, 2023

Medicare is health insurance for those age 65 or older in the U.S. Those covered by their employer's health insurance will have to decide which plan works best for them and their family. One must be enrolled in Medicare before receiving additional private Medicare supplement coverage.

Part A is medical insurance for hospital visits and is for those that qualify. Part B is medical insurance for doctors' visits and other healthcare providers. A monthly premium is charged for coverage. Part D is insurance for drug coverage that's utilized to lower the cost of drugs. One of the requirements of Medicare is the individual will need to work several years while paying into their Social Security and Medicare.

~ 112 ~

Wake Up Action Step: The government will plan for you. They will tax and charge for setting up a health plan on your behalf. Be a responsible adult. Insure your life. Save and invest as soon as possible.

Medicare Part A and B

April 20, 2023

With Medicare Part A and B, there are four main enrollment periods. The initial enrollment period is 7 months, 3 months before, and 3 months after your birthday month. Special enrollment period is for people with coverage through their employer. Those individuals have 7 months after the time they leave the company to sign up for the right plan. However, one can still enroll during the General Enrollment period, which is from January 1st to March 31st of each year. Late enrollment of about 10 percent will be assessed. One must sign up for Part A and B to qualify for Part D.

~ 113 ~

Wake up Action Step: The time one decides to enroll into a plan can have a major impact on the quality of care available. One must take time to understand which plans are available to them and when is the appropriate time to sign up. Never assume anything. Take time today to study the different enrollment dates. Maximize the day.

Medicare Supplement

April 21, 2023

Medicare supplement also known as Medigap is the insurance plan one can purchase for the "gap" that Medicare does not cover, such as deductibles, copays, and coinsurances. The benefits are standard throughout all plans. Whether a person buys from Blue Cross or Aetna, the benefits are the same.

~ 114 ~

Wake Up Action Step: Finding the right plan that is cost-effective is very important, especially for the elderly who for the most part, is on a fixed income. Finding affordable health is important when planning for long-term. Start planning sooner rather than later.

Medicare Advantage: Part C

April 22, 2023

Medicare Advantage is also known as Part C. Part C includes all the benefits and services covered under Part A and B. It can also include Part D. The alternative to the original Medicare is Part C. Health Maintenance Organizations like Kaiser will allow the insured to doctors and hospitals within the network plan. Medicare Advantage plans are typically cheaper. If one wants to go to a specific doctor or specialist, a Medicare supplement may be a better option.

~ 115 ~

Wake up Action Step: Annual election period runs from October 15 to December 7. During this time, one may elect to change their health plan. The cost of health care will only continue to rise. Do what you can today to position yourself for a healthy and productive life.

Long Term Care

April 23, 2023

Long term care (LTC) is a growing problem families must deal with. Those who do not prepare, older children may be forced to quit their jobs to care for their loved ones. Long term care is one of the major types of protection in planning for aging parents. The sooner one sets the proper protection, the better off they'll be.

For those who are 65 and older, 70 percent of the population will need LTC service. For those between the ages of 18 and 64, 40 percent of the population will need LTC service. LTC services are expensive. The average annual cost of a nursing home is $83,580.00 and in Canada it's $47,000.00. The younger the person, the lower the cost of LTC.

~ 116 ~

Wake Up Action Step: Health insurance or Medicare can help pay the cost of immediate medical expenses but not for the LTC of chronically ill people. LTC pays for the insured who becomes chronically ill, which is defined as the inability to perform at two of the activities for daily living. Activities for daily living include bathing, continence, dressing, eating, toileting, and transferring. One can purchase LTC as a stand-alone policy, or as a rider in an insurance policy. Plan for your LTC today.

Estate Planning

April 24, 2023

Estate planning is the process of anticipating and arranging for the management and disposal of the person's estate, in the event the person becomes incapacitated or dies.

Few people take the time to plan, and some individuals believe estate planning is for rich people only. Everyone has an estate, so take the time to build out yours on paper. Estate is everything you own minus debt. Debt can be in the form of a house, car, credit cards, and any other monthly expense. An estate is a tool that helps organize the finances and assets of an individual.

~ ~ 117 ~

Wake Up Action Step: A Will or Trust is a tool that allows a person to organize their wishes and desires as it pertains to their estate distribution when they pass away. Take the time today to start getting your estate in order.

A Will

April 25, 2023

A Will is a legal declaration of a person's wishes regarding the disposal of his or her property or estate after death. A desire, which on a legal document allows one to assign specific items from an estate to a beneficiary. A desire or wish written and documented to assign tangible or non-tangible items from your estate to another person. An Executor can be named in your will. The Executor will perform the wishes of the deceased. Wills also allow the opportunity to choose a guardian for younger children.

~ 118 ~

Wake Up Action Step: Start today to write your Will. No one can figure out your Will for you. If you don't have a will, the government will use a standardized Will to decide how your estate will be distributed. Take 10 minutes to write how you would like your estate to be distributed. If the government distributes your assets, it may not reflect who you are. You owe it to yourself to write out your story, your way!

A Trust

April 26, 2023

A Trust is a contract that gives an individual or an institution like a Bank or Firm the authority to hold legal title to assets while managing the benefits of others. A Trust can help ensure assets are distributed and managed according to the owner's wishes. A Will takes effect after a person dies. Living Trusts are generally revocable, which means it can always be changed. With a Living Trust, all assets like your home, stocks, certificates of deposit, and accounts can be put into a Trust. The Trust can be administered during a person's life and then transferred to a beneficiary after death. Many people name themselves as the Trustee in charge of managing the assets. This gives the owner control and free liberty over the Trust.

~ 119 ~~

Wake Up Action Step: Take control over your future assets and legacy. Having a Trust is like creating a corporation where you can put all your assets. You can run it or have someone else run it for you. Ignorance is a decision. Once you've been provided the information and education, the implementation and execution are the responsibility of the receiving client.

A Trust: Part. 2

April 27, 2023

With a Trust, an individual can name a successor Trustee in case the owner is unable to manage the Trust. A Living Trust may be more expensive to create, fund, or manage than that of a Will. Ensuring a Trust is in place helps avoid probate costs for all the assets in the Trust. One should have both a Will and a Living Trust in place to protect their family. Without having the proper structure in place, one gives room for the government to put one in place.

~ 120 ~

Wake Up Action Step: Proper planning with a professional can be very important in leaving a legacy and preserving an estate. Take control of how you want your story to be written. Do not allow your life's work to be controlled and managed by any outside force that doesn't represent your best interest. Protect the work you have built today!

Saving Futures and Building the Present

April 28, 2023

Create a plan of action and make any necessary changes. Take charge of your future. One of the most powerful gifts that a person has is the ability to choose. One can completely change their lives by simply deciding to do so. Wealth is created and maintained by the way someone thinks. The mind allows one to think and grow rich. There are a small number of things in our lives we have absolutely no control over.

~ 121 ~

Wake Up Action Step: We all can perceive and determine how we'll use the experiences that have happened to us to better ourselves. If one wants to make real change, admission of an issue must occur. Have your family and friends hold you accountable in this area. They typically know you best. It takes courage and maturity to acknowledge an issue and change it.

Manage More, Waste Less

April 29, 2023

Proper management is needed for building a solid financial foundation. A financial professional may not properly be able to help a person who spends more than they earn. Today's economy has changed. Getting a "good job" and working until retirement is no longer an efficient retirement plan.

In today's economy one will need to be more resourceful in how they go about their finances and wealth creation. Working overtime, getting a second job, and working part time are all great starts, but ultimately may not be enough to create the wealth needed to comfortably retire.

~ 122 ~

Wake Up Action Step: Great management allows increased access and assets. Many successful companies were created in the garage or basement of many working-class people. Some businesses started as a hobby and some as an interest, but what every single successful company has in common is that they started. Start today and see where tomorrow takes you!

Manage More, Waste Less: Part 2

April 30, 2023

Make it your mission to change your family's future. There are seven success principles that can guarantee financial success:

a. Increase monthly cash flow. The more cash flow generated monthly can increase opportunities and access
b. Cut down on expenses and spend less. It's not about how much you earn, but more about how much you can keep
c. Manage and reduce debt and liabilities. Compounded interest on debt can interfere with money goals and long-term wealth accumulation
d. Learn and understand how money works

~ 123 ~

Wake Up Action Step: Take time to learn and understand how money works.

a. Learn how to make money work on your behalf.
b. Develop a financial goal. Set up a plan of action that works for you. Be responsible. Your responsibilities are yours. Take ownership of them with the proper plan and protection.

Manage More, Waste Less: Part 3

May, 1, 2023

Saving requires discipline. Start small and increase gradually and consistently.

a. Change unhealthy habits. Challenge your mindset. Embrace change and expect success. Read books that add value to your life. Roll with the winners. Spend time with people that can add to your mindset in a positive way. A better environment will help provide better thinking and solutions.

b. Health is wealth. Without good health, money is useless. Above all things, take care of yourself. Love yourself enough to invest into your body, mind, soul, and spirit. Make time to exercise. Your body is a temple, so maintaining and maximizing it is your responsibility.

~ 124 ~

Wake Up Action Step: Expect to succeed. Winning or losing is determined over time. Execute and follow through with things you start. Get out of your comfort zone. See the world and experience different places. Study a culture other than your own. Remember, you're somebody; you do matter; you're loved and appreciated; you're great!

Food for Thought

May 2, 2023

Nearly one billion people entered the 21st century unable to read a book or sign their name. Over three billion people live on less than three dollars a day. Almost 80 percent of the world lives on less than 10 dollars a day. It's estimated 22,000 children die each day due to poverty. In 1960, 20 percent of the people in the world's richest countries had 30 times the income of the poorest at 20 percent, in 1991, 74 times as much. Wealth is largely determined by location and mindset.

~ 125 ~

Wake Up Action Step: Wealth is power. We can empower the world through the eradication of poverty. Financial literacy is for all people. Everyone deserves a fair chance at wealth creation and accumulation. Education, health, and well-being can all be dramatically improved with wealth. The best way to position your community for success is to empower, inspire, and educate the people. Love and care for people. Ultimately, everyone was put on earth to serve in a particular area and niche. Send love and kindness to everyone you meet. Start giving today.

Poverty is the Root of all Evil

May 3, 2023

By basic definition, poverty is the state of one who lacks a usual or socially acceptable amount of money or material possessions. Poverty is said to exist when people lack the means to satisfy their basic needs. Poverty is not limited to just finance or money. One that lacks the ability to fulfill basic mental, spiritual, emotional, psychological, and physical needs is also poor. The lack of vision and insight for one's life and purpose can also lead to an impoverished and unproductive life.

~ 126 ~

Wake Up Action Step: Work to improve yourself (overall value) by at least 1 percent every day. That means, work to learn one thing daily. Complete one task daily that will help you move towards your goal and destiny.

MAXIMIZE YOUR MOTIVATION

Build with Believers

May 4, 2023

To build a strong and fortified foundation, it's important to build with individuals that believe in the cause and the overall mission. Allow the right pieces to naturally fit into the right spaces and areas. Never force a round peg into a square hole. The best time to start building was 20 years ago! The second-best is right now. Go in confidence and start building with other believers!

~ 127 ~

Wake Up Action Step: Start today to invest in healthy and productive relationships. Take 10 minutes today to call or speak to a loved one. Let them know you love and appreciate them.

Celebrate Your Loved Ones

May 5, 2023

Appreciate and celebrate your loved ones while they're still alive, and while they can feel it. No one truly knows how long they have here on earth. Our time is numbered, so it's important to express yourself to people that matter the most, while you have the opportunity. Communicate how you feel to them today. Tomorrow is not guaranteed.

~ 128 ~

Wake Up Action Step: Celebrate a loved one today. Do one thing for them that they will appreciate.

Finding and Filling Purpose

May 6, 2023

The only true indicator of success or failure is the ability to find and fulfill purpose. Purpose is the reason for which something is done, created or for which something exists. A successful life therefore is not determined by resources, family, or outside influences. A life with accurate function and intent creates a successful life. Finding purpose requires focused and planned actions.

Be clear on your goals. Find out your natural abilities and competencies. Whatever you can do with the least amount of effort is your gift or talent. Combine your gift with your interests while applying consistent focused and planned action. Purpose cannot be fully mastered without effort. Apply, fulfill, and accomplish your purpose today!

~ 129 ~

Wake Up Action Step: Plan out one focused and planned action today that will lead you to finding and fulfilling your purpose.

Opportunity + Preparation = Good Luck

May 7, 2023

There is no such thing as luck! The concept some may believe to be luck is the exercise of preparation within an opportunity. Preparation is the action or process of making ready or being made ready for use or consideration. Create a plan through preparation. Organizing and structuring your day with goals, and a manageable checklist can create opportunities that may seem like good luck.

~ 130 ~

Wake Up Action Step: Use 30 minutes today to create a checklist for your goals. Plan how you will use the next 24 hours to plan and prepare for your success. Start now!

Speak and Manifest Your Reality

May 8, 2023

The ability to speak can create and manifest life. Speech is one of the most undervalued skill sets. When you speak about your life, a standard is set. The ideas that are stored in the mind move to the next phase of development. Once concepts are conceptualized into words, the subconscious mind works to bring resources and tools that can implement the thought into reality.

~ 131 ~

Wake Up Action Step: Speak positivity over your life today! Speak and repeat the following: I can, and I will. I will, and I must. I must, and I manifest. I manifest, and I am destined for greatness and success. Start today to speak life!

Choose Purpose

May 9, 2023

Every day is an opportunity to choose purpose. Purpose is something that can't be forced. You must choose to maximize your life daily. Choosing the highest version of yourself requires self-love, discipline, and follow through. What's your life's purpose? Take time to design and order your life's blueprint. Choose you. Invest in your highest self through your work and planned action.

~ 132 ~

Wake Up Action Step: Schedule 15 minutes today to write out your life's blueprint. What will be your life's work? What will be your life's mission? Write down five areas of your life you would like to see accomplished. Start today. Choose Purpose!

You are Kept for the Problems You Solve

May 10, 2023

You are kept for the problems you solve and let go for the problems you create. Wealth follows value. The key to creating and maintaining opportunities is the ability to find and solve problems. Problem solvers are opportunity creators. Take a step back and ask yourself if you're a problem solver or a creator. Solvers are creators!

~ 133 ~

Wake Up Action Step: Think of one problem you have in your life today. Create a list of three potential solutions and implement one of them. Don't worry if it works or not. Less talking, more action!

Assets over Liabilities

May 11, 2023

Everything in life can be put into two buckets: assets or liabilities. Increase assets and decrease liabilities. Assets are things that add value to you, while liabilities take from you. Assets can be in the form of a relationship or resource. Value attracts the right assets. If you're unsure if something is a liability or an asset, analyze the overall energy of the resource. After everything, did it add to you, or did it take from you?

~ 134 ~

Wake Up Action Step: Assess your relationships and materials today. Categorize each item accordingly. Make the necessary adjustments. Choose assets!

Elevate Past the Status Quo

May 12, 2023

Whoever conforms to the status quo is respected locally, but whoever can change and improve the current systems will be championed and respected for years to come. To change the current state of one's life, one must acknowledge where they are deficient.

Some may want to see positive change in a particular area, but without actively engaging the current state of things, it's almost impossible to move things forward. Once you've engaged, implement fresh and innovative ideas that can improve your life.

~ 135 ~

Wake Up Action Step: Write a list of three things you'd like to change. Commit today to improving in that area. Ask yourself, did I improve in that area today? Make the proper adjustments one day at a time. You can do this!

Build, Plan, and Execute

May 13, 2023

Never allow anyone to talk down on your work, business, or hustle. They don't put food on your table or pay your rent when it's due. Honest work is respected, and yields profit over time. Hold your head high and know you've actively planned and exerted effort for something. Not everyone is privileged with the opportunity to work, so be forever grateful. Maximize any and every opportunity!

~ 136 ~

Wake Up Action Step: Take pride in your work. Walk in full confidence that the work you do will bring value to the marketplace.

Poverty Is the Absence of Self-production and Improvement

May 14, 2023

Poverty is the state of lacking. Any area that lacks production or improvement is poor. As human beings, we are positioned to be a resource. We are created with the ability to create and produce. The more we can produce in a particular area, the wealthier we might become. In short, the resources we manage will properly yield a return on investment. Multiple streams of ROI increase the opportunity and probability of success.

~ 137 ~

Wake Up Action Step: Produce and self-improve today. What's one way you can become more productive today? Choose an area today and commit to improving it. No excuses!

Value Is not Based on Personal Assumptions or Biases

May 15, 2023

Value is not based on personal assumptions or biases, but on the needs and demands of the marketplace. The opinions of others should not dictate or control the value one brings to the marketplace. The needs and wants of supply and demand determine the value of a product or service.

~ 138 ~

Wake Up Action Step: Establish your value. Set a standard and work to improve every day. Decide today to maximize your value. Maximize everything!

The Life You Want

May 16, 2023

The life you want is on the other side of hard work, strategy, and diligence. You can hope, wish, and pray, but without planned and focused work without a strategy, you can almost guarantee failure. The life you want is out there and you deserve the life you desire. Life is 90 percent of what happens to us, and 10 percent how one reacts to it. Position your life properly with the right plan and strategy.

~ 139 ~

Wake Up Action Step: Use the first 30 minutes of the day to visualize the life you want. Write down what you see.

You do Not Get What You Deserve in Life

May 17 2023

You only get what you're willing to negotiate. Many opportunities are lost because of the lack of effective communication. The ability to speak and efficiently communicate ideas and strategies can take a person to the next level holistically.

~ 140 ~

Wake Up Action Step: Practice speaking out about the life you want to live today. Speak to your highest self. Write out a detailed plan for your desired destination.

No One Really Cares about Your Sad Story

May 18, 2023

No one really cares about your sad story. Hustle harder and hustle smarter.

Success favors action and those in motion. In a perfect world everyone would be successful. Success gravitates to those that act over an extended period. Less talking and more action.

~ 141 ~

Wake Up Action Step: Work towards a short- and long-term goal each day. Write down one strategy that'll bring you closer to your goals.

Action over a Period of Time Creates Confidence

May 19, 2023

Confidence increases competence and competency with action improves results. Mastery of results guarantees success. Talk less, more action. More action, more confidence. More confidence, more competence. Increased competence, increased results. Increased results, increased success.

~ 142 ~

Wake Up Action Step: Increase your confidence today by committing to more planned and focused action.

Value Is the Highest Form of Transfer

May 20, 2023

Value is the highest form of transfer. Build, keep and maintain healthy, fruitful, and productive relationships. Value can be defined as the idea that something is held to deserve - the importance, worth, or usefulness of something.

The most important asset you can pass along is information. Generational wealth has more to do with ideas, concepts, and strategies rather than capital resources. Share your wealth of knowledge.

~ 143 ~

Wake Up Action Step: Find one person today that you can be a resource to.

Choose Those Who Choose You

May 21, 2023

Choose those who choose you. How you start means absolutely nothing if you're unable to finish and follow through. Feed and keep those who add value to you. Subtract those that consistently take. Maximize your time and life by aligning with those who want to naturally align with you. Be sure to choose your highest self. It's on you!

~ 144 ~

Wake Up Action Step: Make a list of five things important to you. Find two people in your life currently or someone you have access to, and challenge yourself to cultivate a richer, healthier, and a more productive relationship with them.

Celebrate Life While You Have It

May 22, 2023

Celebrate life while you have it. There's a finite amount of time here on earth, so live while you're alive. Celebrate the opportunity of the day every day. When life is enjoyed and celebrated, you can develop a perspective of appreciation and gratitude. Enjoy and celebrate your life today.

~ 145 ~

Wake Up Action Step: Choose one positive area you have improved in. Celebrate your accomplishment(s) today! Schedule your celebration today!

Growth and Development Is the Highest Form of Self-love

May 23 2023

Growth and development are the highest form of self-love. The most important love in this world is self-love. When you take time to grow and develop as a human being, you say yes to you. Personal growth and development are a key indicator of self-love. The best way to love and care for others is to develop and grow. The better you become as a person, the better you can be for others.

~ 146 ~

Wake Up Action Step: Track your progress. What are the areas that you struggle in? Create a sheet detailing those areas that you are struggling in. When creating your daily life sheet, be sure to date each day to view your progress. Start and execute today!

Personal Belief Can Take You Places Money Cannot Afford

May 24, 2023

Monetary success is important but having and maintaining character and integrity through the process is more important. More important than that, is personal belief. Personal belief gives you the license to accept those good things that are for an individual. It's the fuel that ignites the stored fuel and energy. Without it, the journey of success never truly starts. Above all things, believe in yourself - believe in the highest version of you.

~ 147 ~

Wake Up Action Step: Speak the reality you would like to see in your life. Write out in detail where you see yourself in one year. Write out where you see yourself in five years. Write the vision and make it plain.

Trust Your Instincts and Go After the Life You Deserve

May 25, 2023

Instincts can lead you to your purpose and life's work. Natural ability and skill in a particular area without much effort is an indicator of gifting and opportunity. Go after the life you deserve. You owe you the highest version of yourself.

~ 148 ~

Wake Up Action Step: Figure out the skill or natural ability you do best. Focus on one gift, for one year straight. As time goes on, work to add other complimentary skills as your main gift continues to grow and thrive.

Be Your Own Superhero

May 26, 2023

No one is coming to save you, so it's up to you to save yourself. Develop yourself in as many areas as possible. Save yourself from a mediocre life. The best way to predict a future is to create one. Build your life one brick at a time and don't skip steps. Each season of life is here for two reasons: a blessing or a lesson. Embrace the process. Be the friend, the leader, and the superhero for yourself.

~ 149 ~

Wake Up Action Step: Write down three characteristics of someone you admire and respect, and work to improve in those areas daily.

Just Being a Good Person is Not Enough to Be Successful and Effective

May 27, 2023

Life requires more than being nice or politically correct. A strategy and a focused plan must be created and executed to ensure lasting success. The sharper the plan, the higher the probability of success. Action and follow through must be activated with a plan and strategy.

~ 150 ~

Wake Up Action Step: Create a game plan for success today! Strategize on how you plan to create a fulfilling life. Find an accountability partner that will hold you responsible for your goals. Win big today!

There Is No Substitute for Provision

May 28, 2023

You need a strategy; you need a plan and phenomenal execution. Provision is the action of providing or supplying for something. The ability to provide has less to do with charisma or strength, but rather the capability to create a strategy and game plan for life.

Phenomenal execution and follow through is required. What will be your main source of income? How will you be able to diversify your income streams? Be sure to address these questions in detail when choosing the life for you.

~ 151 ~

Wake Up Action Step: Determine today you will grow and solidify your main source of income. Analyze your main source of income and add two streams of income from that one source. Wake up and shake up your finances today!

Blame Yourself. Figure Yours Out

May 29, 2023

The difference between a dream and your reality is work and follow through. Take accountability for every area you might be lacking in. Even if you have not been positioned to win, figure out how to play the cards of life more effectively. There are people with far less than you, but they've managed to play their cards better while also elevating their life.

~ 152 ~

Wake Up Action Step: Write out where you are right now. Record the ways you have contributed to your current position and state. Determine three areas you need to work on and commit today to aggressively work on those areas.

Be Your Natural Self

May 30, 2023

Allow the right opportunities and people to connect and manifest. By being your most authentic self, you allow the right people and opportunities to connect and manifest. The road to you can be a journey but commit to the process of self-discover and remain encouraged along the way. Allow yourself to connect with your natural interests and instincts.

~ 153 ~

Wake Up Action Step: List three activities you enjoy. Schedule some time in your weekly schedule to incorporate one of those activities into your routine.

The Most Important Real Estate to Maintain and Invest in Is Your Body

Your body allows you the platform to live and exist. Proper maintenance of self-yields the highest results and return. The ability to properly manage self allows for clarity of purpose and thought. Take care of your real estate, and your real estate will take care of you.

Wake Up Action Step: Invest in you today. Take inventory on your current life. Write down the areas that negatively impact your body. Remove them from your life today. Be serious with your health. Start now!

Be Productive

May 30, 2023

Outcome and results outweigh unproductive talk and opinions. The best way to respond to self-doubt is with intense, consistent, and focused action. Results always speak the loudest. No matter how much is debated, results communicate value in a unique way. Productively produce products and services. In the end, only the producers are remembered.

~ 154 ~

Wake Up Action Step: Commit to producing today. Your life depends on your ability to produce. Create a list of productive actions. See yours through.

Market and Brand Yourself

May 31, 2023

It's impossible to support and endorse what you don't know. Visibility can take your product or service places skill cannot. Many times, we choose professionals based on accessibility and convenience. Take time to market and brand yourself. Proper marketing and branding can exponentially grow and expand your company. Unfortunately, we live in a world where perception is held higher than reality. Who you're perceived to be can be regarded as more important than who you are.

~ 155 ~

Wake Up Action Step: List out the ways you're currently marketing. Increased actions lead to increased opportunities. More practice and effort in any area dramatically increases the probability of success and mastery.

Be a Pro in Real Life

June 1, 2023

Professionalism is consistently achieving high standards, both in the work you do and the way you behave. Many attribute the word professional with athletes. Being a professional is more than the sport an individual plays. People can become proficient in any given area with enough focused training and effort. The character of a person can also become professional as well. Become a professional in real life!

~ 156 ~

Wake Up Action Step: Become a professional in real life today. Focus on an area you would like to become more proficient. Write out why you want to improve in this area. Set a schedule to dedicate 15 to 30 minutes growing in this area. Start building today!

The Most Important Person to Communicate to and with Is Yourself

June 2, 2023

Effective communication begins with self. The more honest you are with yourself, the more effective you become with communicating with others. The ability to communicate internally sets the standards. Many times, the way you communicate with yourself is the way you'll communicate with others. Practicing healthy and consistent communication skills enables one to improve and increase their capacity to communicate.

~ 157 ~

Wake Up Action Step: Practice healthy communication skills today. Speak positive affirmations in the mirror while you're brushing your teeth. Repeat: I am great. I am blessed. I set the tone for today. I choose excellence. I choose love. I choose peace. I choose me!

Elevation Requires Separation

June 3, 2023

To increase and advance to the next level, it's important to take time to self-assess. The more time you have to process and digest information, the more perspective is gained. There's a finite amount of time for an opportunity. Understand the timing and season of opportunities and relationships. Maximize the opportunity during the allotted time period. Always look to grow the opportunity into something much bigger than what was initially given.

Never look at where it began, but rather what it can potentially turn into with enough watering and nurturing. With the right amount of touch and care, a seed can turn into a forest. Never despise humble beginnings. Embrace the process. This is where the action happens!

~ 158 ~

Wake Up Action Step: Write down the three largest opportunities in front of you today. Within those opportunities, list how you can grow and maximize those opportunities. Maximize each opportunity!

Attack the Day with Constant Action

June 4, 2023

More action, less talking. The more action we exhort on an activity, the higher the probability for success. There is no substitute for action. Experience is not read or sold in a book. The best way to ensure results is to practice the act of action. Success is attracted to things in motion. Action tells people that you're willing to invest in your beliefs. The day must be seized. Implement action in your life today.

~ 159 ~

Wake Up Action Step: Start your day with action. Plan to incorporate two activities into your daily routine that will move you directly towards your goals. Practice the art of action. Action more today. Talk less today.

Starve Any and All Distractions

June 5, 2023

Feed your priorities. The most dangerous weapon is a loaded and focused mind. Magnifying your goals while minimizing roadblocks will ensure a faster and more productive journey. Consistent action over a period of time creates momentum and leverage. Ask yourself, which is more important instant failure or delayed success? You attract what you focus on. Put the focus on you. Soon the focus will become you. Elevate your game by downplaying the distractions.

~ 160 ~

Wake Up Action Step: Determine the four areas that distract you the most. Draw four quadrants on a piece of paper. Input one distraction in each of the four boxes. Underneath each box, list four ways to avoid the distraction. Feed your priorities today!

Stay Offensive

June 6, 2023

Offense in sports is engaging an opposing team with the objective of scoring points or goals. Live life on the offense. Score and aggressively pursue your goals and dreams. Some things just don't happen. For every accomplishment there's usually hours of sacrifices. Remain in motion. It requires less energy to add to the momentum of an object that's already in motion as opposed to igniting and starting an object from nothing.

~ 161 ~

Wake Up Action Step: Attack the day. Start the day with consistent and focused action. Plan the action of the day. Act on three of your goals. Write out three ways you can improve from yesterday.

Know Your Value Then Charge Tax Plus Interest

June 7, 2023

Understanding personal value is one of the most important tools in being successful. Take time to self-assess every area of your life. What areas are you naturally gifted in? Determine your value. Never allow anyone to determine who you are. The moment you communicate your value is the moment you set the standard for how people will treat you. Never settle!

~ 162 ~

Wake Up Action Step: Write out your three most valuable skills. How were you able to determine these three traits? Work to improve in these areas daily. Practice communicating your value daily!

Love, Appreciate, and Celebrate Your People While They are Alive

June 8, 2023

Love, appreciate and celebrate your people while they can feel it. No one truly knows the number of years they have on earth. Many times, people delay expressing themselves under the assumptions they have tomorrow to express their love to a loved one. Don't delay the expression of love. Practice love and appreciation daily.

~ 163 ~

Wake Up Action Step: Wake up with a sense of gratitude. Ultimately, no one owes you anything. Send out three text messages or calls that express love and appreciation daily.

The Most Important Investment Is Yourself

June 9, 2023

Investing in stocks, real estate, or any other investment vehicles outside of self is always secondary in value and return. Personal improvement is necessary to maximize one's life and purpose. Adding marketable skills while improving holistically will position one to excel in real life. Build and invest in the life you desire. Be willing to invest in resources that can yield tangible life results today.

~ 164 ~

Wake Up Action Step: Describe three areas where you can self-improve. Write down three reasons you believe it's important to self-improve. Commit to self-improvement.

Keep People Around You That You Can Invest into

June 10, 2023

Investment is the commitment of an asset to attain an increase in value over a period of time. The purpose of investing is to generate a return from the invested asset. Investing in people can yield the largest returns. Investing in the right people can protect and insulate an individual. Two forces working in unison can accomplish significantly more than one. Harness the energy of others. Harness the energy of self.

~ 165 ~

Wake Up Action Step: Roll with the winners. Surround yourself with people who can add value to your life. Take inventory of the people in your life today. Write down five individuals who currently have the most influence on your life.

It's Not about how You Start but How You Finish

June 11, 2023

Starting means absolutely nothing if you can't finish and follow through. The art of finishing can create momentum and velocity for an individual. Motion leveraged properly can be used as a catalyst for success. Start building today. Practice finishing. Visualizing the end goal at the beginning can help keep priority.

~ 166 ~

Wake Up Action Step: Create a 3-6 month vision board. Where would you like to be in six months? What are the practical daily steps that must be taken to achieve that goal? Create your vision board today.

Champions are Built for the Road Ahead

June 12, 2023

Build your life to last and endure to the end. Many people move throughout their life and only compete. Becoming a champion is one of the most important goals on the road to success. Focus on the lane ahead. Plan and prepare with the proper tools. Understand the mission. Project the amount of time and effort needed to accomplish a goal.

~ 167 ~

Wake Up Action Step: Champions are built to last. Write three goals you want to accomplish. For each goal, write the amount of time you think it would take to accomplish that goal. Write out the tasks that must be achieved to complete the mission. Study what's needed to win and carefully move forward towards your victory.

How You Finish

June 13, 2023

Starting means absolutely nothing if you can't finish and follow through. Planners are winners. Faith without works is ineffective and dead. Finishers are winners. Learning the ability to complete projects creates confidence. Confidence overtime improves performance. Every winner is a finisher, and every finisher is a winner. Get in the habit of finishing what you start.

~ 168 ~

Wake Up Action Step: Exercise the art of finishing. List the areas in your life you feel are under construction. Create deadlines and set a timetable to complete each task. Write the vision and make it clear. Win big today! Win in everything!

Winners Win! Win Big! Win in Everything

June 14, 2023

Winning is a lifestyle. Every day is an opportunity to win or lose. Your dreams mean absolutely nothing without a plan. Each morning you wake up is an opportunity to become a winner. Choose your path and plan your way. Act on your convictions. A winner never quits, and a quitter never wins. Never settle for short term wins. Leverage the wins and capitalize on every opportunity.

~ 169 ~

Wake Up Action Step: Look in the mirror and repeat: I am a winner, I win big. I win in everything. Affirm your highest self today!

More Action, Less Talking

June 15, 2023

Talk is overrated. Action is required to move from one level to the next. There is no secret to success, you must do the work -action must be used. Action is like fuel to a vehicle. You can plan the destination, but without the proper fuel, the ultimate destination may never be reached. The more supply provided, the more refined the resource. Utilize action more in every activity, project, and goal. Act before action takes you.

~ 170 ~

Wake Up Action Step: Practice action in motion. In 2-3 sentences write out your goals for the year. Write out one action step that can be taken daily to move you toward your goals.

Making Choices are Easy if You're Prepared for the Consequences

June 16, 2023

What makes decisions difficult are the consequences. Studying the pros and cons of every decision prior to making a choice allows one to move forward with full confidence. Faith and fear cannot remain together. Have faith as you move through your journey. Strategically plan your way. Any and everything can happen. Anticipate up-and-coming traffic and debris. Understand the obstacles and move accordingly.

~ 171 ~

Wake Up Action Step: When deciding, think through all possible scenarios. Understand that nothing is truly guaranteed in life. Study the consequences and move in confidence.

Not Knowing Is Not an Excuse

June 17, 2023

Ignorance is the root of all major issues. Life is governed by laws and principles. Not understanding and practicing life principles does not negate the validity of the concept. Not understanding the law of gravity doesn't stop gravity from pulling down an object once it's thrown up into the air. Gravity will still work to push the object back down, regardless of how the object feels about the air. This same principle can be applied to all areas of life.

~ 172 ~

Wake Up Action Step: Do not make excuses. Spend time learning key life principles. Study high achieving successful individuals. Take note of key characteristics and apply accordingly.

Know Your Life Blueprint. Have a Life Plan

June 18, 2023

Tomorrow starts today. It's important to know the blueprint you have for your life. Where do you see yourself in the next five years? Where do you want to be personally, professionally, and/or academically? Start saving the necessary funds today to position yourself tomorrow. Plan out the vision with planned and focused action. Start with what you have now and leverage your position for a higher level.

~ 173 ~

Wake Up Action Step: Write out your vision and make it clear. Plan a 3-5-year game plan for your life. Write out daily, weekly, and yearly steps necessary to accomplish your goals. Write how your personal goals are connected to your professional and academic goals. Start to build and plan today!

Remain Solid and True to Self. Life Has a Funny Way of Rewarding What's Real

June 19, 2023

Truth is the only thing that will stand the test of time. The truer you are with yourself, the more freedom you can experience. Nothing can be hidden forever. True substance always finds a way to the top. Life is cyclic. Whatever you put into the world will be returned in a different form of energy.

~ 174 ~

Wake Up Action Step: Write down three core characteristics of yourself. What's something you would not compromise no matter the circumstance? Compile a list of things you enjoy doing. The more honest you are, the more impactful. Write out the things that make you the most authentic version of yourself.

Give Thanks and Gratitude

June 20, 2023

Take time to embrace those who add value to your life. Good people who are genuine and have your best interest are rare. Embrace those who embrace you. Celebrate those who celebrate you. Building with the right people can make your work a lot more efficient and more effective. Work smarter, not necessarily just harder. Giving thanks opens opportunity for more grace. Fill the cup that fills you. Always give thanks and gratitude. Tomorrow has a funny way of rewarding grace and gratitude.

~ 175 ~

Wake Up Action Step: Either call or text one person a day and let them know you appreciate them. Do not assume they know. Start today and put gratitude to practice. Truly no one knows tomorrow. Be thankful for today. Forgive yourself for yesterday. Be grateful for life.

Appreciation of Assets Increase Access

June 21, 2023

Access to opportunities will generally increase assets over time. An asset is any resource owned or controlled by a business or economic entity. It's anything used to produce positive economic value. Assets represent the value of ownership that can be converted into cash. Great management of assets is a form of appreciation. Access to capital is a key to building wealth. If someone believes in you enough to invest capital into you, how you manage that opportunity will speak volumes.

~ 176 ~

Wake Up Action Step: Wherever you find yourself in life can be improved and elevated. Never take the failures of life personal. What happened has been done. What are you going to do about it? What steps are you going to take to advance your life to the next level? Ask yourself the tough questions today to improve your tomorrow.

Stay Where You are Celebrated

June 22, 2023

Move from where you are tolerated. Life is too short to be in an environment where you are not tolerated. Celebrate people while they are still alive. Waiting to celebrate people is unwise and poor practice. When people are celebrated, they are more inclined to do more. Begin with a simple thank you. Give people their flowers while they are alive and can feel it. Develop a spirit of thankfulness and celebration.

~ 177 ~

Wake Up Action Step: Celebration is key, so learn to celebrate life more. Take 10 minutes today to celebrate 10 areas in your life that have improved. Write down 10 things in your life you are proud of. Call or text one person and let them know you're proud of them.

Fortitude Is Needed

June 23, 2023

Remain steadfast in your convictions even when faced with inconvenience and tough times. Persistence outweighs resistance. Fortitude refers to the strength in facing adversity or difficulty. Fortitude is the emotional ability to withstand adversity. Build a strong mindset. Positive self-talk can help build character.

~ 178 ~

Wake Up Action Step: Love yourself enough to forgive yourself. Maintaining the right perspective in every situation can open many opportunities. Stay the course. Never allow negative talk to overcome the positive areas in your life. Write and speak 10 positive affirmations over your life daily. You are blessed beyond measure. Claim and own this truth.

Complain Less, Solution More

June 24, 2023

Being solution driven creates more opportunity for success. Don't waste energy on complaining about a problem. The same amount of energy one uses to complain can be directed towards finding the solution to that same issue. It's not how you start; it's how you finish. Finishing requires focused energy and effort. Closing a chapter in something can be rewarding. Finishing also improves self-image and confidence.

~ 179 ~

Wake Up Action Step: If you're unable to finish, it's better you never started. Don't start anything that can't be completed. Be a master of completion. Finishing things increase confidence. When you can finish in one area, it gives you a base and foundation needed to see things through to the end.

Live and Embrace the Moment

June 25, 2023

Nothing is truly guaranteed. Move past the past. The only time guaranteed is right now. The past has happened, and tomorrow is not promised, so make the most of today; make the most of every day. Maximize the time you are given.

~ 180 ~

Wake Up Action Step: Work as if today is your last day on earth. Remain encouraged. Life tends to get better over time.

The Sun Will Set

June 26, 2023

No matter the wave, the sun will still set. Our time here on earth will eventually come to an end. If death is certain in life, we all should plan accordingly. Believe and work towards your highest self. Protect your assets. The most powerful resource one can pass down to their children is information.

~ 181 ~

Wake Up Action Step: Giving money, capital and resources are all important, but if a group of people is not financially literate, wealth will always gravitate towards where it's properly managed.

It's You vs. You Everyday

June 27, 2023

There's only one true competitor, and that's you. The only enemy is the one inside. Learning the power of self-reflection and discovery will unlock a new world for you. If you can go to bed a better person than when you woke up, that day is a success.

~ 182 ~

Wake Up Action Step: Give yourself grace. You're doing the best you can. Study the areas you are weak in and apply your energy in improving those areas. Start small and record your journey. Find an accountability partner to hold you responsible. Maximize the day every day. You owe you.

Faith More, Fear Less

June 28, 2023

Fear and faith cannot share the same space together. One must take precedence over the other. Faith is the complete confidence or trust in a person, thing, or concept. The more trust someone has in something, the more likely they are to give to it. Lead by faith. Exercise your faith by enduring tests and trials. Tests and trials will help grow and strengthen your faith over time.

~ 183 ~

Wake Up Action Step: The best way to deal with fear is to confront fear head on. If there's something that needs to be done, but is causing you fear, make a swift decision and act. Action over time can cancel fear.

Invest in Tomorrow

June 29, 2023

The best way to determine tomorrow is by creating it. The best way to create tomorrow is through a focused and determined plan. Planning and execution can guarantee a productive and successful future. Take time to write out the future you want and deserve. Writing down goals and plans allows a person to maximize on opportunities.

~ 184 ~

Wake Up Action Step: Start investing today. A sharpened sword can cut down a tree quicker than a dull blade that's repeatedly used. Investing a sound and solid education and skill set can take you much further. Building a solid skill set will pay dividends over time.

More Action, Less Talking

June 30, 2023

Talk is cheap. Talk alone is not enough to move things forward. To speak without any real plan or goal is simply babbling. Actions qualify talk. The more action, the more powerful the words. Live by example. Work to accomplish the goals at hand. Never assume anything. Action improves competence.

~ 185 ~

Wake Up Action Step: Build strong habits through action over time. A habit is a routine of behaviors repeated regularly and tends to occur subconsciously. Habits determine our focus and desires. Take 10 minutes today to write out your habits and routines. You may be surprised by what you find out.

A Special Purpose

July 1, 2023

God has a special purpose just for you. If you're reading this you are loved, and God has a special purpose just for you. Remain encouraged and replace uncertainty and doubt with planned and focused action. Finding and fulfilling purpose unlocks the keys of destiny.

~ 186 ~

Wake Up Action Step: Study who you are as a person. What can you do naturally well? What areas are you naturally good at? Focus and develop those areas. Expanding your natural abilities is where your strongest and most promising opportunities are located. Use ten minutes daily to develop your natural gifts and talents.

More Life, Success, Peace, and Prosperity

July 2, 2023

Life is too short to waste a second being unhappy and not content. Never take anything in life too personal. People rarely do things for isolated reasons. Many behaviors stem from internal manifestation. If possible, be at peace with all people. Peace allows for self-reflection and self-discovery.

~ 187 ~

Wake Up Action Step: Many of the world's brightest and most impactful ideas were birthed from a place of solace and serenity. Never underestimate the power of peace of mind. One of the sweetest gifts here on earth is peace of mind. I wish you much success and prosperity.

Build and Establish Lifelong Relationships and Brands

July 3, 2023

Your network is equal to your net worth. Who you know does matter. The relationships you build can add or subtract from your life. Everyone we meet in life is either a blessing or a lesson. Take inventory of everyone in your life. Where do they fit in your life? What areas do they contribute?

~ 188 ~

Wake Up Action Step: Understanding where people fit will give you grace to be patient with them. People will eventually disappoint you at some point. Understanding people are naturally limited in their abilities and capacity will allow for grace and patience to be extended.

Cherish the Moments

July 4, 2023

Nothing is ever truly guaranteed. You can do everything right in life and still be disadvantaged. You could go to the right schools, have the right friends, and even land the perfect job, and still lose it all in a matter of seconds. Good fortune is not equivalent to good behavior. Cherish the good times. Good times don't last forever. Bad times don't last forever. A grateful and thankful heart can be cherished forever.

~ 189 ~

Wake Up Action Step: Take five minutes from your busy schedule to cherish the moment. Look at where you are currently. Reflect on where you were and look at where you are currently. Your progression is a blessing worth cherishing.

Build with Believers

July 5, 2023

The ability to build with people that believe is powerful. Belief inspires you to produce your best work. Being surrounded by people who genuinely love you and have your best interest is a game changer. Never underestimate the power of love and self-belief.

~ 190 ~

Wake Up Action Step: Everyone must start from somewhere. It is not where you start, rather it is where you finish. Build with believers and finish strong. If you want to get there quickly, go alone, but if you want to go far, go together.

Enjoy the Process

July 6, 2023

Be sure to enjoy the journey along the way, and the final destination. Typically, the most impactful and fruitful lessons are the ones learned on the way. During the process, character and integrity are being built. Also, during this process, patience is also being built. To test gold, silver, and other precious metals, it must be tried and tested under specific degrees of heat. The specific melting point of each individual precious stone will determine the contents of the mineral.

~ 191 ~

Wake Up Action Step: The same thing applies to your life. Trials and tests only come to our lives for one reason, which is to reveal who we are to ourselves. If you falter under pressure, that's an indicator of who you are. Tests expose the type of material you're made of.

Write Your Own Story

July 7, 2023

Be sure to be an author of your own story. Define and write your own story, your way. People will try to write you off. There's a tendency to label things and place them into boxes. The reality is that human capacity cannot be caged or properly measured without understanding individual purpose and destiny. The beginning of a thing does not have to be the same as the ending of a thing.

~ 192 ~

Wake Up Action Step: Wake up every day with the understanding you hold the keys to your destiny. Free will has enabled the ability to choose and determine for self. I control the keys to my destiny. I control how my story will end. With a stroke of a pen, destiny can be written and determined.

Results over Opinion

July 8, 2023

Results ultimately cancel opinions. An opinion is a view or judgment formed about something, not necessarily based on fact or knowledge. Results are consequences, effects, or outcomes of a thing. An outcome can be measured, tried, and tested. By something being tested over time, the contents of a thing are put on display. Capacity can be determined and measured. If something can be measured, it can be improved.

~ 193 ~

Wake Up Action Step: Results speak louder. When you focus on results you allow yourself to grow and improve. By focusing on results, you give yourself the best opportunity to be successful. Control what you can and ignore what you cannot. Start growing today!

Invest in Yourself

July 9, 2023

Invest in your highest self each day. Every day we wake up, we must choose which version of ourselves we will show up for today. By saying yes to the project of self-development you are saying no to anything less than your highest self. Take steps every day to grow and move forward.

~ 194 ~

Wake Up Action Step: A journey of a thousand miles starts with one step. One step towards the right direction is a huge step towards progression. The goal of life should be progression, not perfection. Constant progression overtime can improve most all situations. Start your growth and process today. You can do it!

Welcome to a Fresh Chapter of Opportunity

July 10, 2023

Welcome to a fresh chapter of opportunity - a fresh chapter of opportunity and potential. There are endless opportunities contained in 24 hours. Great entrepreneurs, artists, athletes, and world changers all have the same number of hours in each day. The difference between someone being great with their time is how it's utilized.

~ 195 ~

Wake Up Action Step: Some take stock of their hours and deploy their time into positive and wealth building activities. Others waste their sun rises on unproductive activities. In the end, who is to blame? A person is given the luxury of choice. May you maximize every second on earth. May the force be with you!

Live, Invest, and Progress

July 11, 2023

Capitalize on every opportunity presented. Live life while you can. Many people are alive but never live. A life void of purpose is a waste and lacks true depths and meaning. You owe it to yourself to understand your life's work and how it fits into God's overall plan for your life. Invest in information, skills, and people that can add value to your life.

~ 196 ~

Wake Up Action Step: Make constant progression a life's mantra. Study the flow of your life. Which areas do you struggle in? Find an expert in that area, partner with that expert, and compensate them for their help. Feed every good thing that's feeding you.

Plan, Create, and Build

July 12, 2023

Plan, create, and build out the life you desire. No one is coming to save you. There's no large red easy button in life. Whatever you refuse to resolve will manifest and grow. Create the lifestyle you desire through increasing your revenue streams. Every willing and able person should have at least four revenue streams. Living and operating with only one revenue stream is the equivalent of gambling. One source of income says "I hope and wish everything goes perfect. I refuse to plan, and indeed I have planned to fail with only one income source."

~ 197 ~

Wake Up Action Step: Build out the proper infrastructures to enable constant success that can multiply and exponentially grow over time. Build a T.E.A.M. Establish a group of people who think alike and share similar values and principles. Build out a platform everyone can participate in and start delegating and building today.

Let Your Work Speak

July 13, 2023

Only what's real will stand the test of time. The power of life and death is in the tongue. Some people have been removed from this earth based on the words that have come from their mouth. On the other hand, some have built generational wealth by speaking things into existence. Speak life with every opportunity. One kind word can literally make someone's day and or week.

~ 198 ~

Wake Up Action Step: The most positive thing you can do for someone is speak life over them. Being good to people pays a dividend that continues to pay overtime. Love people and use money. Use the money and love the people. Start loving people more today!

Shine Bright Regardless

July 14, 2023

No matter how hard it's snowing, trust and believe there's someone benefiting from the cold and ice. Be sure it's you! Life is simple about perspective. What angle are you observing from? Take a step back from every situation and ask yourself, does this situation require my immediate attention, and can my time be better spent? By taking inventory of your time and associates, you can leverage and maximize every opportunity.

~ 199 ~

Wake Up Action Step: Managing opportunities well create more opportunities for the future. Never allow the influences from your environment to hinder you from growth and self-development. Only you can control the true power change or stay the same. Choose higher. Grow your mindset today!

Exercise Your Purpose

July 15, 2023

To exercise any area, one must concentrate on a specific group of muscles and apply focused action in that area over a period of time. This is like exercising life's purpose. If you desire to have an effective life's purpose, you must first find and develop a personal life's purpose and know which areas to focus on.

~ 200 ~

Wake Up Action Step: Know the value and skill set you bring into the environment and never allow your gifts and talents to be exhausted or abused by anyone or anything. Exercise your purpose in every given opportunity. Use the gift. Release the gift. The true beauty of a gift is found in its utility. Start using what's inside of you. Everything you need is inside of you.

Consistent Action Equals Success

July 16, 2023

Repetition over an extended period of time guarantees improved and increased performance in any given area. Again, more action and less talking! Constant action will eventually improve performance. Action allows for practice and progression. Even if things don't happen the way you expect them to, never give in or give up. Success is a process and comes in stages. In fact, initial success and prosperity may first come in the form of failure.

~ 201 ~

Wake Up Action Step: Failure teaches us valuable lessons that help expand our vision and perspective. It's up to you to use or abuse the seeds of failure. Continue to attack the issue head on. Don't run away from problems. Instead, embrace them as a gift and opportunity.

Learners are Earners

July 17, 2023

Learners are Earners. Readers and leaders. Information is now the new currency. Applied information can change and dramatically improve most situations. Some individuals may feel as though learning ends after graduating from a university. If you study great people throughout life, they've worked and studied outside of the confines of a college but branched out to the lifestyle of being a lifelong learner. Life becomes much more enjoyable when learning and principles are applied daily. Don't sell yourself short. You deserve the best version of yourself.

~ 202 ~

Wake Up Action Step: Keep an open mind. Many things we may be searching for can be found within our reach. Self-reflection is necessary and studying things that will add joy and happiness to our lives can be very beneficial and valuable. Use today to study the things most impactful to self. Promise yourself you'll dedicate your life to being a learner for a lifetime.

Learners are Earners.: Part 2

July 18, 2023

The more you know, the more marketable you become in the market. We live in an information world. Hard labor does not guarantee monetary success. Those who think and plan will be best positioned to take advantage of the new world of information. Take a course in something that interests you. The reason the mechanic commands the price is because he understands when your vehicle isn't functioning correctly; the mechanic has taken time to study the principles of automobiles.

~ 203 ~

Wake Up Action Step: A good mechanic will stay updated with the changes in vehicles. They will continue their education in the study of cars to stay relevant, up to date, and competitive. The principle of continued education can be applied to our lives. By staying informed in life, one can take advantage of opportunities and areas of life that are available to the prepared and positioned. Start today to work towards the life of continued and consistent life learning.

Roll with the Winners

July 19, 2023

Surround yourself with people who add value to your life. Subtract and add accordingly. Listen more, talk less. One of the fastest ways to become a winner is to surround yourself with proven winners. Surround yourself with people who have become winners. A consistent winner applies key principles that enable them to win.

~ 204 ~

Wake Up Action Step: Don't assume winning long term is a function of luck or chance. Mere chance has no relationship with a planned and focused long-term winner. Start today and decide you will be a winner.

Roll with the Winners: Part. 2

July 20, 2023

Being surrounded by winners allow you to pick up on key habits that enable the culture of winning. You can study a losing team and a winning team, and the one clear difference between the two will be the company's culture.

Winners do not tolerate excuses and irresponsibility. Winners understand and practice the principle of action and follow through. Winners tell themselves, "I can. I will not stop until the mission is complete."

~ 205 ~

Wake Up Action Step: Winners understand a loss is no loss at all, but rather a lesson to be studied and embraced for future performance. Love yourself enough to be patient with yourself. Rome was not built in a day. Great things take time to develop and progress. Remain encouraged, today is the start of a beginning.

Fix Your Vision

July 21, 2023

Some things break your heart but fix your vision. Keep going. Heartbreak can be one of the strongest forces in developing purpose and character. Disappointment forces you to take a hard look at yourself. You can only take responsibility for your life. Embrace the heartbreak and take it as a restart. A chance to reset yourself is important. One could be driving and speeding in the wrong direction.

~ 206 ~

Wake Up Action Step: Direction is higher than speed. Many drivers are on a highway, going nowhere. A crash-course to their missed destiny. Take time to properly plan and organize your steps and route. Along the way, type G-O-D into your GPS and get prepped for your overflow season. Remain encouraged. Remain blessed.

How Much You Manage to Keep

July 22, 2023

It's not about how much you make; it's how much you manage to keep. There are many high earners that have more expenses than income. Until income and cash flow are higher than expenses and debt, true wealth may not be created. Filling a large bucket with water that has a hole at the bottom will create the same results over time no matter how much water is poured in the pocket.

~ 207 ~

Wake Up Action Step: It is better to clog up the leaking hoes than to exhaust strenuous energy in trying to over fill the bucket. Excess follows great and efficient management. The better a person is at managing an area, the higher the probability there will be an increase in that area. Guarantee your success by applying key management principles into your life today.

Maximize Your Day

July 23, 2023

Don't make excuses. Maximize your day! Take inventory of how you're living your life. Create a life's blueprint that aligns with your goals and objectives. Build out the life you deserve. Develop systems and processes that can be utilized daily.

~ 208 ~

Wake Up Action Step: Taking the time to build out structures can save you time, money, and effort in the long run. Bet on yourself. Your best life is on the other side of dedication, commitment, and focused passion.

You Can Do It

July 24, 2023

Own the day. Win the day! Believe in your day because it's on you, and you can do it! If you can think it, you can achieve it. The very thought of a possibility qualifies the reality of its existence. Do not underestimate the power of an idea and phenomenal will. Focus and drive have created countries, industries, and economies. We are created to create.

~ 209 ~

Wake Up Action Step: The sooner we start perfecting the art of creation, the sooner one can live an unlimited life. Self-belief unlocks faith. Self-love allows one to receive the love of another. Start today by working on yourself

Knock Out the Excuses

July 25, 2023

Nothing fruitful has ever been produced with excuses. Kill The complaints. Excuses have never paid a single bill. The reality is everyone is going through their personal storms. Some may have a yacht, a sailboat or may even be drowning and struggling to stay afloat.

~ 210 ~

Wake Up Action Step: Be kind with everyone you meet. Encourage people as best you can. Do what you can for yourself. People are more inclined to help people that are putting forth the effort. Consistent effort over time can yield large results.

No One Is Coming to Save You

July 26, 2023

No one is coming to save you; I can promise you that. Go out there and fight for the life you deserve, the life your kids deserve, and the life this generation deserves. There's a specific problem in this generation you were handcrafted to solve. The way you were designed is perfect and purposeful. Our natural interests and passions all align with our predestined project and work.

~ 211 ~

Wake Up Action Step: Go in full confidence. Our success and prosperity in life is tied to our destiny. Start where you are at. Grow where you are planted. Do not wait to begin. No one knows the exact amount of time we have left on earth. Utilize each precious second to develop your natural gifts and ability. Use every minute to build out your destiny and future.

Are You Vibrating Higher?

July 27, 2023

Inflation is here. Everything is going up. Gas prices are up. The cost of milk and eggs are up. But what about your life? Is the value you bring to the marketplace going up? Has your mindset or skillset gone up? What about you? Are you vibrating higher? Investing in yourself will always yield the highest return over time. Investing in your health and mindset can position you to a lifetime of success and prosperity. Take mental health seriously! Take mental wealth seriously!

~ 212 ~

Wake Up Action Step: Poverty chases money. Money chases wealth. Wealth chases value. Become the value you desire. Value is chased and pursued by every other category. Increasing personal value can dramatically increase and improve your experience here on earth. Inflate in real life.

Peace Is the Highest Form of Self Love and Care

July 28, 2023

Above happiness, love and joy, peace is the highest form of self-love and care. Encompass every good thing from within and protect your peace by every means possible. No matter what it costs you, never sell the currency of peace of mind. Peace is too high of a cost to comprise. The degree in which you love yourself is determined by how much you love yourself.

~ 213 ~

Wake Up Action Step: Self-love gives you a lens to view love from others. Protect the things that bring you authentic joy and peace. Our passions give us a vehicle to express ourselves. The ability to release is essential for survival. Built up anger and hatred can cause cancers and decline. Do yourself a favor let it go and grow through it.

Winners Win

July 29, 2023

Winners win! To win, you must apply, position yourself to receive, and practice. Use your foundational wealth to build generational wealth for yourself and for your future. Winning is a mentality. Winning is an attitude. How you do one thing sets the stage for how you will do other things. Take pride in your work. Be able to defend your work in the face of trouble. Do not allow others to talk down on you. Understand that success is just a process.

~ 214 ~

Wake Up Action Step: Failure is not a destination, but an exercise of faith. A loss is a lesson before the blessing. Some people will walk away from their blessing in the middle of the process. Go through it. If you've endured this long, be sure to reap the rewards of your labor!

Money Does Not Solve Money Issues

July 30, 2023

If you want more of anything in life, manage what you have better and more effectively. Great management allows for more access and opportunities. If expenses are higher than your income, they'll be a deficit carried out monthly.

~ 215 ~

Wake Up Action Step: Including interest and taxes on top of a negative balance of each month could bring the possibility for money issues. There are two main ways to increase income. The first is to decrease the amount of debt and expenses carried on a month-to-month basis, and the other is the amount and number of income streams created and generated on a month-to-month basis.

Money Does Not Solve Money Issues: Part. 2

July 31, 2023

The easiest way to increase income is by multiplying and increasing the cash flow from original streams of income. Instead of trying to work additional jobs for increased income, look for ways to increase the pay scale from your original income streams.

~ 216 ~

Wake Up Action Step: Think of additional products and services that can be offered to clients and added with current strategies. Study the needs and gaps of the industry. What needs have you observed that you can fulfill? On the other side of problems, there are opportunities to build wealth through solutions.

Action and Follow Through

August 1, 2023

Winning is an action step. Action and follow through is what separates a "would've, could've, and should've" from an actual winner. Maximize your blessings! How you manage your gifts may determine how much access and opportunities you receive in the present and future.

~ 217 ~

Wake Up Action Step: If you want more of anything in life, manage what you have better and more effectively. Study your results. There is always room for improvement. Find an accountability partner. Assign someone in your life that can always be honest with you. Iron sharpens irons.

Assets or Liabilities

August 2, 2023

Everything in life can potentially be put into two buckets: assets or liabilities. Increase your assets and decrease your liabilities. An asset is something that could generate cash flow, reduce expenses, or improve sales. All assets can be classified as current, fixed, financial, or intangible.

~ 218 ~

Wake Up Action Step: An asset is a resource with economic value an individual, corporation, or country owns or controls with the exception it will provide a future benefit. A liability is something a person or company owes, usually a sum of money. Liabilities are settled over time through the transfer of economic benefits including money, goods, or services.

Assets or Liabilities: Part. 2

August 3, 2023

Liabilities are completely different than assets. Liabilities refer to things that you owe or have borrowed. Assets are things you own or are owed...putting money into your pocket. Liabilities are things that take money out of your pockets monthly. The name of the game is to increase assets and decrease the number of liabilities monthly.

~ 219 ~

Wake Up Action Step: Acquire assets as soon as possible. The more assets under control and management, the more leverage a person possesses. Assets can produce cash flow. Cash flow is more important than cash itself. Unfocused and unplanned cash can become a liability. Put your money to work for you today!

Take a Shot

August 4, 2023

Get in the game. You miss 100 percent of the shots you don't take. You can never truly know your potential without attempting. Many attempts can help build character. Through the process one can create a clearer vision and focus. Never despise humble beginnings. Celebrate the shots taken.

~ 220 ~

Wake Up Action Step: Be encouraged to take more attempts. The opportunity of a lifetime is on the other side of chances and probability. You can increase your chance at success by taking calculated and focused shots. Always fail forward.

Become the Fruit You Desire

August 5, 2023

Clear your way by cutting down all distractions and debris. The road to success requires focused action and follow through. Plant and plan your way today. The garden of surplus begins with a seed. Sow seeds of success, prosperity, and longevity. Plant the seed, and water it accordingly. Tend and cultivate your garden.

~ 221 ~

Wake Up Action Step: If there are weeds growing, pull out the unproductive areas, and insert and keep productive and fruitful fruits. Manifest and work towards your highest self. You woke up today, another day that was not guaranteed. Another day that was not promised. Another day that no one owes you.

Create the Sunshine You Want to See

August 6, 2023

Create the sunshine you want to see in the world. He has risen. The price has been paid. Be forever grateful. Be forever thankful. Maximize today. Appreciate the day. Peace, love, and prosperity. Weather the tides of life with an optimistic and strategic outlook. No season lasts forever.

~ 222 ~

Wake Up Action Step: Think and be grateful. Water and nurture a healthy and productive mindset. There is a sea of opportunities waiting for those who act and remove excuses. The right mindset can dramatically change an experience. Start creating a life you will never need a vacation from.

You Owe You Your Highest Self

August 7, 2023

Your highest self will require discipline, sacrifice and dedication. Dedicate the next six months toward working to build yourself in every good area. The best return on investment is an investment in self. Do the self-work. Ultimately, we attract who we are. The best way to find a good friend is to first be friendly.

~ 223 ~

Wake Up Action Step: Become the change you want to see. Live by example. Allow your life to speak on your behalf. How you love and care for others is largely based how you love and care for yourself. Start with yourself and work yourself out to the others. Start today and make yourself the number one priority, because truly, you are!

Multiply Your Value in Real Life

August 8, 2023

Multiply your life by 10 times, every 10 years. Growth over time is a powerful tool. God is great. Become a living breathing example of God's faithfulness. Be thankful for everything. The next 10 years will be legendary. Start today and build. The best Investment is in self. Focus on self.

~ 224 ~

Wake Up Action Step: Challenge your mental, physical, emotional, spiritual, and personal stability. Be a student of self-discovery. The more understanding and clarity one can have of self, the better they are at making decisions.

Celebrate Your People

August 9, 2023

Celebrate people today and every day. The reality is no one truly can predict tomorrow. Take time to let your loved ones know you love and appreciate them. Ensure they know you care for them. Spend quality time with those who matter the most. By investing time into your loved ones, you communicate to them they matter and are loved.

~ 225 ~

Wake Up Action Step: Stop making excuses. Time waits for no one. Spend at least 10 minutes a day telling a loved one how much you love and care for them. No one knows when the last time may be the last time.

Work to Graduate Throughout Life

August 10, 2023

The ability to start and finish a chapter is worth celebrating. Work to graduate throughout life. Success is the ability to graduate from one season to another. Graduation season is upon us. Sleepless nights, papers due, applications and interviews. Be a student of life. A graduate of progression.

~ 226 ~

Wake Up Action Step: Study different areas of your life. What areas have you had long term success in, and what has contributed to the success? Improve the areas that you struggle in. Expand on the things that you do well. Strengthen your strengths and downplay your weaknesses. The confidence you develop from execution can improve virtually every area of your life. Start building today!

Play to Win

August 11, 2023

In the end, we'll all be stories. Enjoy life no matter the circumstance. Ensure that your life is hydrated. Play to win. Play for keeps. Life is one big playground. Every decision you make will either take you closer to your goals or further away. Master the art of decision making. People perceive perceptions partially.

~ 227 ~

Wake Up Action Step: Maintain the right attitude and perspective in every situation. You can outthink any obstacle with the right perspective and vantage point. You are born to win. Live like it! Play your part!

Invest with Winners: The Winning T.E.A.M.

August 12, 2023

Tired of losing money? The stock market is crashing. Accounts have been in the negative for months. Ask yourself, what can I invest in? You need to invest in a Winning T.E.A.M. You need to learn how to start a business. Become financially literate. Are you tired of losing? Want to learn how to invest like a winner? Then, bank with the winning T.E.A.M. Invest with winners.

~ 228 ~

Wake Up Action Step: Build out a T.E.A.M. of achievers, executors, and leaders. Learn from people that have produced results for themselves. Learn about personal and business taxes. Learn about business credit. The best investment is in self! Financial Literacy is a must!

Learners are Earners

August 13, 2023

If you're comfortable where you are and don't want to grow, then continue to do you. You've been educated. Maximize your gift. Make the most of your talents. The best way to appreciate what you've been given is by utilizing and maximizing everything you have been given.

~ 229 ~

Wake Up Action Step: Tomorrow is not guaranteed. Start today. Start now. Best of luck. Do what you need to do for you. Life is designed to give a solution before a problem. We all have a sad story. Work harder. Work Smarter. Learn more, earn more. Make it happen!

Chase Your Dreams or Your Nightmares Will

August 14, 2023

Chase your dreams or your nightmares will! We are given a specific window to accomplish our goals, dreams, and purpose. Dreams are given to help refocus vision and mission. There is nothing the mind cannot bring to reality. Dream big and dream often. Take heart and remain encouraged. Things tend to happen at the right time. Don't rush your process. It's your process for a reason.

~ 230 ~

Wake Up Action Step: The pain from not pursuing true purpose and passion outweighs the risk and feeling of failure. Give yourself an honest shot at something before moving on. Patience must be paired with consistent and direct action. Take heart, for the marathon of life, is not for the faint hearted.

Chase Your Dreams or Your Nightmares Will: Part. 2

August 15, 2023

Even if things never happen the way you envisioned, there are many opportunities and people you will meet on the way to destiny that can contribute to your ultimate life's journey. Hard work, consistency and never given up is the ingredients for sustained success.

~ 231 ~

Wake Up Action Step: Just keep going! It is all about the work you put in during Practice! Keep putting in the work. Once you put in the work do it constantly over time it becomes like second nature just like muscle memory. Make success a habit. You are a born winner. Winning is already inside of you!

Where Winners Actually Win

August 16, 2023

Never lose sight of the goal and objective. We are here to improve the lives of ourselves and others in a positive way. Celebrate the small wins. Leverage the small wins into bigger wins. Maximize every opportunity. Work as if the opportunity in front of you may never come again. Honestly, it may never come back. Embrace the moment. Map out exactly what you want from every opportunity and relationship.

~ 232 ~

Wake Up Action Step: Manage your expectation by understanding people are human, and because of their nature, they are bound to disappoint at some point of time. If you're honest with yourself, you can admit you may have also disappointed another person. Be kind to yourself. Be kind to others.

Invest a Seed

August 17, 2023

Many times, people wait until funerals to celebrate their people. Today we will celebrate our people right now! The harvest of tomorrow is the seed you plant today. If you do not plant today do not expect a harvest tomorrow. We will invest a seed into every artist represented today. We are showing you love, as you have blessed us today.

~ 233 ~

Wake Up Action Step: The quality of the seed will manifest in the quality of fruit. Determine today that you will sow productive and meaningful fruits. How you treat yourself and others are all tied to the fruit you bear. Decide today. Only you can control your process. Make it happen.

Invest a Seed: Part 2

August 18, 2023

Become invested in yourself. Your life can completely change in one year. Invest in something that can bring tangible value back into your life. Time is an exhaustible resource. We have a limited amount of it. Be clear and specific when allocating energy and efforts. Once time is spent, it is resource that can never be reclaimed no matter the amount of capital.

~ 234 ~

Wake Up Action Step: Limit your accessibility. People tend to decrease the value of things that are easily reached or obtained. Place value on the things that are important to you. You have the power to determine what something is worth. You have the power to determine value. Determine your value and move accordingly. Start building today!

Invest a Seed: Part 3

August 19, 2023

How did you invest your money? How someone invests their money speaks to who they are and what they value. Start early to invest. Investing tends to improve over time. Investing is a game of numbers and time can dramatically improve the probability of success.

~ 235 ~

Wake Up Action Step: Do not invest in things you do not understand. Take time to study the areas you would like to invest in. By taking time to study within an industry, you can maximize returns over an extended period time. Study and find yourself approved.

Invest a Seed: Part 4

August 20, 2023

Land will always appreciate over time. With the correct information, you can leverage money and invest in income producing properties that cash flow every month. By buying and holding, you position yourself for short and long-term gain. After collecting rental income over a span of a few years, you can develop equity appreciation. You can now sell the property for a net return. The capital gains earned can now be reinvested into another property. Invest to reinvest.

~ 236 ~

Wake Up Action Step: Investing is a cycle. By the learning the principle of investing one can enjoy the fruits of return and profit. Keep your eyes on the prize and remain encouraged.

Speak Life. Live Life

August 21, 2023

Determine the life you desire to live. Think through the kind of lifestyle important to you. Be specific on the things you want to manifest. After you decide the direction, in which you desire to pursue, align your behaviors with those desires. Look at the activities you are currently engaging in.

~ 237 ~

Wake Up Action Step: Does those activities put you closer or further away from the life you've decided to live? Plan, commit to a decision, and never look back once a decision has been determined. Determine today what matters most to you and start working towards your best life. You owe you your highest version of yourself. Work to educate and elevate.

Choose Higher

August 22, 2023

Choose a life that's higher. Live life with more abundance.

Impact the lives of others in a positive way. Celebrate your journey. Write out five positive things you love about your life. Deliver a high quality, positive and impactful message every day.

The way you choose to live your life is a ministry. Always choose higher! Indecisiveness is a decision. Be decisive in the way you conduct your life. Move towards your destination with full confidence and joy.

~ 238 ~

Wake Up Action Step: The most important investment is yourself. Keep people around you that you can invest in as well. Investment into people yields the highest form of return. You can positively impact a while generation of people based on the quality of investment that is sowed.

Direction Is Higher than Speed

August 23, 2023

It's not about how you start, but how you finish! Starting means absolutely nothing if you're unable and unwilling to finish and follow through. Champions are built for the road ahead. Many drivers are on a highway to nowhere. A crash-course to missed destiny. Take time to map out your destination. The quality of your plan can take you places talent alone cannot reach. Learn to work smarter, so you can grow and go further

~ 239 ~

Wake Up Action Step: Take time to properly plan and organize your steps and route. Be sure to type G-O-D into your GPS and get prepped for your overflow season. Remain encouraged. Remain blessed.

Real Is Rare

August 24, 2023

Good people who genuinely have your back and love you regardless of the circumstances are rare, so cherish them. They are God's gift to you. Spend less time with liabilities. Appreciate the "real," because real is indeed rare.

~ 240 ~

Wake Up Action Step: This season we celebrate those individuals in our life that add value to it. Take every opportunity to uplift and celebrate people. Love and appreciation can improve most relationships. Love more and express yourself clearly and intentionally.

Enjoy Your Life

August 25, 2023

Enjoy your life while you can. Enjoy it with the people who matter to you the most. Celebrate your loved ones while they are here. Love, appreciate and, celebrate your people while they're still alive and can feel it. Maximize your gift. Make the most of your talents. The best way to appreciate what you have is by utilizing and maximizing.

~ 241 ~

Wake Up Action Step: Tomorrow is not guaranteed, so start enjoying your life today. Don't listen to the naysayers. Do what you need to do for yourself! Life is designed to give a solution before a problem.

Increase Your Demand

August 26, 2023

Your demand is based on the number of problems you solve. Take the next six months and invest strictly on skills, assets and information that increase your value. Manage what you supply and increase your demand.

~ 242 ~

Wake Up Action Step: Do the internal work. No one is here to save you. Study yourself and make the necessary corrections. All work yields return over time. The value you develop internally directly correlates the value you bring to the marketplace.   Increase your income by improving your outcome.

Rewrite Your Narrative Your Way

August 27, 2023

You can rewrite your story your way! No one can control your story but you. With every new day, there's a new opportunity to rewrite history. Think about who you would like to become. Work towards making your vision a reality every day. Write out your goals and make it plain. Add to your story every day.

~ 243 ~

Wake Up Action Step: Consistency and focus can create any reality. Write as if your life depends on it. Use today to define what you believe in. Write out what is important to you. Write out your legacy. Write and live out your life on your terms.

Harder Work than Hard Work

August 28, 2023

Working smart and working hard requires dedication. But you know what's harder than hard work? Laziness, being broke, and not being able to contribute to your family. There's a price one must pay to become successful and effective, but there's a higher cost associated with living a mediocre life that does not produce.

~ 244 ~

Wake Up Action Step: The internal pain of settling for a life beneath you is far more threatening than the idea of working hard and smart. Take great pride when you find yourself working smarter and harder to build a life that will produce. Weeping may endure in the night, but the sun will shine in the morning.

Love or Hate

August 29, 2023

Your kids may either love or hate you based on the decisions you make. No child ever asks to be brought into this world. The life we'll inherit tomorrow is largely based on how we manage the life we are living today. The first step towards fulfilling your purpose in life is to take full responsibility for the life you're living.

~ 245 ~

Wake Up Action Step: The success or failure of life is in your hands. Some situations are harder than others. Free will is the ultimate equalizer. Decide the kind of life and legacy you will leave for your loved ones.

You Only Get What You Are Willing to Negotiate

August 30, 2023

The life you desire comes from hard work, strategizing, and through being diligent. Start negotiating today, you'll get there. You don't get what you deserve in life if you aren't willing to negotiate. No one really cares about your sad story. Hustle harder, and smarter. Success favors action and those in motion.

~ 246 ~

Wake Up Action Step: Do not despise humble beginnings. Everyone must start somewhere. Learn to leverage experiences whether good or bad. Every negative area in life can be redeemed into something positive and productive. Go in full confidence today! Remain blessed and encouraged.

MAXIMIZE YOUR MISSION

All Honest Work Is Respectable and Yields Return

August 31, 2023

Build, plan, and execute, and never allow anyone to minimize your work, business, or hustle. People won't feed you or pay your rent when it's due. Honest work is respectable, and yields profit over time. Embrace your process even if takes you a few years to finally arrive to your destination; the results and satisfaction of finishing something will be well worth it.

~ 247 ~

Wake Up Action Step: Become a finisher. Completing your mission can be rewarding. Finish well and be consistent. True talent can never be denied. Go out there and make it happen. You can do it!

Be Your Own Superhero

September 1, 2023

Growth and development are the highest form of self-love. Personal belief can take you places money cannot afford. Money cannot buy confidence or class. Confidence must be built from within. Attack the areas in your life that give you the most fear. Building confidence requires a commitment to face challenges and obstacles. Faith and fear cannot exist and operate together, you must choose one. Trust your instincts and go after the life you deserve. Guaranteed, no one is coming to save you! Save yourself. Be your own Superhero!

~ 248 ~

Wake Up Action Step: Just being a good person is not enough to be successful and effective. There is no substitute for provision. You need a strategy, a plan and phenomenal execution. Start building out the life you deserve today.

Figure Yours Out

September 2, 2023

The difference between a dream and your reality is work and follow through. Do the personal work to make your dreams become a reality. Figure out the areas and needs, in which you're lacking in. Take inventory of where you are in life currently. Biasness and false opinions cannot improve you.

~ 249 ~

Wake Up Action Step: The more direct you are with yourself, the more direct you can be with others. The more transparent you are with yourself, the more transparent you can be in life. You got it, so make it happen. Remain blessed and encouraged.

Be Your Natural Self

September 3, 2023

Allow the right opportunities and people to connect and manifest. Life has a funny way of rewarding and uplifting what's real. Commit to becoming and maintaining your authentic self. There is no better feeling than becoming successful while being yourself. And there may be no worse feeling than becoming successful by being someone you're not.

~ 250 ~

Wake Up Action Step: You owe yourself your most natural self. People around you deserve to know the real you. Be real with yourself. Live by example. Your natural self will attract the right people in your life. Trust your process. You got it!

Maintain and Invest in Is Your Body

September 4, 2023

The most important real estate to maintain and invest in, is your body. Proper maintenance of self-yields the highest results and return. Health is true wealth. All the money in the world means absolutely nothing if you're not in good health. Budget your energy. Create a working priority list in your head daily.

~ 251 ~

Wake Up Action Step: Write down the things most valuable to you. Make time for your life and health. You can never be so busy you neglect your health. Perform one healthy activity daily. Commit to a better and healthier you today!

Results Cancel Opinions

September 5, 2023

Become more productive. Outcome and results outweigh unproductive talk and opinions. Focus on activities that are productive and yield positive return. Focus on results. By managing your results and how you react to outside noise, you can position yourself for long lasting success and prosperity.

~ 252 ~

Wake Up Action Step: The reality is someone will always have something to say. Do not be deceived by wasteful ideologies and concepts. If you have a solid game plan, and the necessary work ethic and follow through, you'll accomplish the necessary results.

Elevation Requires Separation

September 6, 2023

Recognize when it's time to move away or towards a relationship. If a relationship is not feeding you or adding directly to the quality of life you enjoy today, it may be time to disconnect. Separate from liabilities and increase your skill set and asset class.

~ 253 ~

Wake Up Action Step: Understand the timing and season of opportunities and relationships. There is a specific window and time frame to accomplishing goals. Do your part in seizing your day. Your time is now. Go in full confidence.

Attack the Day with Constant Action

September 7, 2023

Attack the day with constant action. Estimate how much energy is needed to accomplish a goal and multiply the effort by at least 10. Always be in motion. We live in a world that rewards momentum. Momentum is mass in motion. Objects and ideas can have mass and movement.

~ 254 ~

Wake Up Action Step: Leverage the success you have in one area and transfer that to every other area of your life. Consistent action overtime creates momentum and leverage. Starve all distractions. If it does not feed you, remove it.

Feed Your Priorities

September 8, 2023

Who are the people and things that feed you? Protect those areas in your life by any means necessary. What feeds you is for you. Do not assume those around you understand and appreciate what brings you peace and joy. Cherish what is yours and move in complete confidence.

~ 255 ~

Wake Up Action Step: Take it one day at a time. The most dangerous weapon is a loaded and focused mind. Remain consistently offensive. Engage your opponents with an objective of scoring points and goals in life.

Faith with Work Works

September 9, 2023

Faith with works is effective and productive. Your plan means absolutely nothing without work. Hope is a noble characteristic, but hope alone, is not a proper plan of action. Plan, but have faith and hope that it'll all out work out. Create a structured course of actions that can be clearly defined and applied.

~ 256 ~

Wake Up Action Step: Planners are winners. Faith without works is ineffective and dead. Establish a solid plan and work on a better strategy. Action more and talk less. How you start means absolutely nothing if you're unable to finish and follow through.

True Indicator of Success or Failure

September 10, 2023

Purpose is the true indicator of success or failure. Finding and fulfilling purpose is one true indicator of success or failure. If a laptop is used as a door stopper, has it been properly used to its full potential. While the laptop has been used, is this the highest use of the item? The answer is no! If the laptop is not used as a laptop, the laptop never fulfilled its true purpose.

~ 257 ~

Wake Up Action Step: Choose those who choose you. Feed and keep those who add value to you. Value yourself enough to invest in those things that can help you find and fulfill your purpose. Start building today!

Opportunity Plus Preparation Equals Good Luck

September 11, 2023

Design and create your good luck. Do your part by consistently being in preparation. Maximizing opportunities requires a focused and determined mindset. Opportunity favors those who are positioned and prepared. Look for a chance to exercise skills and capability. Through trials and the testing of faith, character is developed.

~ 258 ~

Wake Up Action Step: Run towards the direction of work and development. Life changing opportunities are typically wrapped inside of hard work and consistency. Embrace the process and attack the future with full confidence. You are a winner. Behave like it!

Being Good Is Not Enough

September 12, 2023

Just being a good person is not enough to be successful and effective. Some people may believe that being a good person is enough to be successful and productive. However, there may be no correlation with becoming effective just by being good. Being good and nice to people is important and should be practiced but being skilled in a particular area requires a consistent and focused commitment to excellence.

~ 259 ~

Wake Up Action Step: One must excel in a particular field to create a life that's truly fruitful and productive. Do not settle for being just good enough. Go after your highest life. Commit to excelling in real life. Build out a life you can take pride in.

Market and Brand Yourself

September 13, 2023

It's impossible to support and endorse what you don't know. There are many unknown talented people with exceptional gifts are positioned to serve the world positively. For example, there's a ton of artwork that's been produced, but never released. Books that have been beautifully written, but no audience to digest and consume its content.

~ 260 ~

Wake Up Action Step: You must learn the art of marketing and promotions. The ability to sell may be one of the most important skills to learn and develop. Most interactions and conversations involve the likely selling of something.

Value Is the Highest Form of Transfer

September 14, 2023

The definition of value is to estimate or assign the monetary worth of something and to rate or scale in usefulness, importance, or general worth. Work to always add value in any area. The ability to maintain value will open opportunities for you in the present and in the future.

~ 261 ~

Wake Up Action Step: The person that consistently maintains and adds to their value will always have a place in the marketplace. Become hard to replace. Increase the value of everything around you by improving and building every day. Start adding to your value today.

Take Action Before Action Takes You

September 15, 2023

You get out of life what you put in. You can only withdraw what you have deposited. Learn to invest more than what you withdraw. Whatever you would like to manifest requires consistency and intentional action. The two things that are constant in life are change and time. Change will happen whether we change or not.

~ 262 ~

Wake Up Action Step: It's important to initiate the change you want to see before change disrupts what you see. Time is moving constantly. Time is something that cannot be controlled but can be managed. Manage your time effectively by planning and directing how it will be used.

Choose to Live Today

September 16, 2023

Choose to live and embrace the moment and the beauty of today. Appreciate yesterday and be excited for tomorrow. Only look back at the past to help build your past. Make peace with your past and leverage negative situations into positivity and productivity. Every single experience can be used and redeemed.

~ 263 ~

Wake Up Action Step: Be kind to yourself. People do the best with what they have. Give yourself the opportunity to grow and expand. Choose to live and not just exist. Many people are breathing, walking, and even talking, but are they truly living Embrace the fact you were given another opportunity at this thing called life. Embrace that you're here today. If you woke up today, that means there is still something left for you to accomplish and fulfill.

Make the Most of Today

September 17, 2023

Don't worry about yesterday or even tomorrow. Focus on how you can maximize each day in front of you. If you can manage your days well, the future will naturally manifest in accordance to how well you are managing today. Today is a gift, hence why today is the present.

~ 264 ~

Wake Up Action Step: Give a gift that keeps giving. Give today and tackle each issue life throws at you one day at a time. Be sure to celebrate your wins. People tend to remember their losses because of the way the loss made them feel. Therefore, it's important to celebrate your wins to remind yourself that progress in indeed being made.

Above the Status Quo

September 18, 2023

Live above the status quo. Status quo is the existing state of affairs, particularly with regards to social, political, religious, or military issues. Status quo can also refer to the current state of social structure and/or values. Live a life above the status quo. Learn to think for yourself. What's important to you? Incorporate the answer into your daily living.

~ 265 ~

Wake Up Action Step: Decide daily to live above. Reach for those things that are higher. Develop healthy and productive habits. Study the current state of things. By understanding the current affairs of things, you can improve and expand opportunities for all people. Start building today.

Gain and Expand Your Understanding

September 19, 2023

Invest time and energy to gain the necessary skills and knowledge base in any field you find yourself in. The more you know, the more you can grow. The more you understand, the more you can expand. Sound judgment and information can be utilized for protection and progression.

~ 266 ~

Wake Up Action Step: Apply your attention to ideas, concepts and strategies that can add value to your life. Start building a life that's respectable and dignified today. Add to your knowledge base daily. Commit to your highest self today.

Live and Thrive by Principle

September 20, 2023

Determine a set of principles you can commit to and live by them. Principle is a fundamental truth or proposition that serves as the foundation for a system of belief or behavior, or for a chain of reasoning. The more disciplined you are with your principles; the easier life becomes. Learn to commit to what you believe in.

~ 267 ~

Wake Up Action Step: Trust in your process. Principles of today can save and build your tomorrow. Consistently build towards your future. Engage your beliefs and challenge your fears. Faith and fear cannot coexist. Choose Faith.

Do Not Waste Your Days

September 21, 2023

Every day that passes is a history we must account for. What are you doing with your days? Is each day being maximized? These are just a few questions you should ask yourself each day. Time is a commodity, that once exhausted, can never be reclaimed.

~ 268 ~

Wake Up Action Step: Free yourself from the pressure of mediocrity and laziness. A little sleep and a little slumber, and poverty will come like a thief in the night. Stay consistent while building a strong foundation. Great things typically take time. Remain encouraged.

Speak and Live Truth

September 22, 2023

Above all else, be truthful with yourself at all times. One can lie to everyone else, but it's not possible to lie to yourself. Ultimately, you know when you are living a life that's beneath you. Take time to discover your truth. Fix your eyes on everything lovely, kind, caring, and beautiful.

~ 269 ~

Wake Up Action Step: Speak truthful words and speak life. Wisdom is more valuable than raw materials. In all that you get in life, make sure to gain understanding with wisdom. Apply useful information in your life daily. Make it a habit.

Lazy Hands Make for Poverty

September 23, 2023

It's no secret being lazy serves no true benefit. A wise person brings glory to their family name through their work and actions. Resources that are stolen will hold no true value in the end. Remain principled in all that you do. Have you ever seen a true giver beg for bread? The principle of giving is that it provides opportunity and resources to the giver.

~ 270 ~

Wake Up Action Step: By releasing what you have, you can make room for what's in store. True giving isn't something that just happens, it's a way of life. True giving is a lifestyle. Follow the giving principle today and remain blessed!

Diligent Hands Brings Wealth

September 24, 2023

Nothing in life just happens. What you put out is ultimately what you will get back. A person that is diligent in his or her work will reap their fruits in due season. The person that gathers crops in the summer is smart and resourceful. The ant is thought as wise because they store and build their stock during the summer. The one who sleeps through summer is thought to be foolish. We have a limited number of years here on earth.

~ 271 ~

Wake Up Action Step: How you choose to spend those years will come down to values and priorities. The game of life rewards planners and executors. Be sure to be on the winning side of life through your constant action and planning. Remain blessed and encouraged!

The Power of The Tongue

September 25, 2023

The power of life and death is in the tongue. The mouth of the upright is a fountain of life. The mouth of the divisive conceals violence. Hatred stirs up conflict, but true love covers many wrong doings. Wisdom and understanding are on the lips of the wise and discerning.

~ 272 ~

Wake Up Action Step: The prudent stores up wisdom and understanding, but the mouth of fools invites personal and community ruin. The results of a life of wisdom and understanding is life. Divisive people conceal hatred with lying lips and spread slander and foolishness.

The Power of The Tongue: Part 2

September 26, 2023

Foolishness is not ended by multiplying words, but the prudent hold their tongue. The tongue of the wise is rare jewels. Their lips nourish and build up many. Wealth and resources follow those that gain understanding and build up their value through applied and tested principles.

~ 273 ~

Wake Up Action Step: From the mouth of the prudent comes the fruit of wisdom. The lips of the upright know what finds favor and life. Pride comes before a fall. Be humble or life will humble you.

A Generous Person Will Prosper

September 27, 2023

One person gives freely yet gains even more. Givers are builders. Withholding what should be given can cause waste and poverty. A generous person will prosper. Whoever refreshes others will be refreshed and renewed. Those who hoard grains or resources in any area of their life bring poverty to themselves. Those that trust in their wealth will fall.

~ 274 ~

Wake Up Action Step: Those who trust in their principles and values will prosper. Don't worry, the fruit of the upright is a tree of life. Both, the wise and the foolish will receive their dues on earth. Make sure your equation of life adds up to the world you would like to live and the person you would like to become.

The Prudent Keeps Their Knowledge to Themselves

September 28, 2023

The fool shows their annoyance at once but the wise overlook an insult. The prudent chooses their friends carefully. A fool's heart blurts out folly. An honest witness tells the truth, but a false witness tells lies. The words from a fool will pierce like a sword, but the tongue of the wise will bring healing.

~ 275 ~

Wake Up Action Step: Truthful lips will live forever but a lying tongue will last forever. Do the right thing and be a good person. Good people promote peace and enjoy life. Deceit is in the heart of those who plot evil. Diligent hands will rule, but laziness ends in forced labor. Remain blessed and stay encouraged.

Hope Deferred Makes the Heart Sick

September 29, 2023

A longing fulfilled is a tree of life. A longing fulfilled is sweet to the soul. Execute and fulfill what you start. Fulfilling and accomplishing projects brings satisfaction and confidence. The more one can accomplish, the more they can excel. Dishonest money dwindles away, but whoever gathers money little by little can make it grow.

~ 276 ~

Wake Up Action Step: Whoever scorns instruction will pay for it. Whoever respects a command is rewarded. Good judgment wins favor, and the teaching of the wise is a fountain of life. Those who are prudent act with knowledge, but fools expose their folly.

An Inheritance for Your Children's Children

September 30, 2023

A good person leaves an inheritance for their children's children, but a sinner's wealth is stored up for the righteous. Whoever fears the Lord walks uprightly, but those who despise him are devious in their ways. An unplowed field produces food for the poor, but injustice sweeps it away.

~ 277 ~

Wake Up Action Step: Real men build generational wealth. Where there's no oxen, the manager is empty. The strength of an ox comes from an abundant harvest. All hard work brings a profit, but mere talk leads only to poverty. Create a plan and build out a life through action and hard work.

A Heart at Peace Gives Life to the Body

October 1, 2023

Those with patience have great understanding, but one who is quick-tempered displays foolishness. A gentle answer turns away wrath, but a harsh word stirs up anger. Always be kind and respectful. You truly never know what someone is going through. The mouth of the wise will spread knowledge. Better a small serving of vegetables with love than a home full of hate.

~ 278 ~

Wake Up Action Step: Appreciate what you have and maximize the use of everything under your management and control. Whoever fears the Lord has a secure fortress, and their children will have a refuge.

Pride Comes Before Destruction

October 2, 2023

Pride comes before destruction - a haughty spirit before a fall. It's better to be humble with the people than to be proud with the oppressors. Whoever gives action to proper instruction will prosper.

~ 279 ~

Wake Up Action Step: Take heart and remain encouraged. Life is not for the faint hearted. It's better to gain knowledge and understanding rather than gold. The right applied information will take you further in life than all the money in the world. Choose wisely. The world is truly yours.

A Friend Loves at all Times

October 3, 2023

True love is unconditional. A brother is born for a time of adversity. Whoever loves quarrels invites their own downfall. Live a cheerful and content life. A cheerful heart is good medicine for the soul. Love covers the wrong of another. One who has unreliable friends will soon be destroyed.

~ 280 ~

Wake Up Action Step: There is a friend that sticks closer than a brother or sister. Wealth attracts many friends, but even the closest friend of the poor deserts them. If you want friends, show yourself to be friendly. Start today to model the person you would like to see in others around you. Live by example today.

A Gift Opens the Way

October 4, 2023

A gift ushers the giver into the presence of the great and upright. The one who receives wisdom, loves life, and cherishes understanding will eventually prosper in life. Ultimately, time and chance will happen to us all, so learn to roll with the punches. Along the way, life will throw some obstacles and challenges in your direction.

~ 281 ~

Wake Up Action Step: Embrace every single situation you find yourself during your process. Whether good or bad, everything happens for a reason. Embrace both seasons. Challenges were placed in your life to grow and develop you. Take heart and remain encouraged. You are a born winner. Live like it!

Plans Are Established by Seeking Advice

October 5, 2023

Before embarking on any major project or business be sure to seek the proper advice and counsel. The plans of the diligent and prudent lead to profit just as surely as haste leads to poverty. Pace yourself during your journey.

~ 282 ~

Wake Up Action Step: Many people are on the crash course to their missed destiny. Whoever loves pleasure will be poor. Be disciplined in all that you do. Build out the life you desire through planned, focused, and consistent action.

Apply Your Heart to Instruction

October 6, 2023

Apply your ears to words of knowledge. The wealthy rule over the poor. Build and accumulate wealth over time. The borrower is slave to the lender. Do not take advantage of the poor because of their disadvantage. Be honest and speak the truth.

~ 283 ~

Wake Up Action Step: Instill a level of discipline in every area of your life. If you drink alcohol, work to become a moderate drinker. Remove smoking from your life. Drink more water daily and reduce your day-to-day stress and or stressors. If you cannot change the problem, let it go and be at peace with your life. Above all else, love yourself and be kind.

Do Not Envy

October 7, 2023

Envy is a feeling of being discontent and having a resentful longing for someone else's possessions, qualities, or luck. There is a future and a hope for all people who have faith and work. Do not wear yourself out trying to become wealthy or rich. Build out a plan you can stick to. There are some people who wish they could experience even your worst day.

~ 284 ~

Wake Up Action Step: Each person is given what they can handle. Become a good manager of what you have no matter how good or bad the position. The better you can manage the position you have, the better the position will become.

Through Wisdom a House Is Built

October 8, 2023

Through understanding, a foundation is established. Through knowledge things of value can be built out and created. Do not expect a fool to want to understand solid counsel. Accept people for who they are, not for who you wish them to be.

~ 285 ~

Wake Up Action Step: The more honest you are with yourself, the more you can be honest with others. Careful guidance and wisdom are needed for true success. Great victory is won through many advisers. Live and choose wisely!

Evil Has No Hope

October 9, 2023

Evildoers have no hope or future. Do not be fearful or anxious of negative people. Move and plan accordingly. If you observe a snake moving don't run, rather position yourself to counter and leverage any and every move the snake may or may not execute.

~ 286 ~

Wake Up Action Step: Accept the fact the snake may have evil intent towards you. Don't waste any time or energy towards trying to change the snake. Use every bit of energy to improve and increase your value in every necessary area.

A Little Sleep, a Little Slumber

October 10, 2023

A little sleep, and a little slumber is all it takes. A little folding of the hands to rest, and poverty will come on you like a thief in the night. The distance between poverty and wealth is relatively small. Someone can be in abject poverty in the beginning of their lives and become wealthy in their later years.

~ 287 ~

Wake Up Action Step: Life is probability and chance. There are some strategies and tactics that dramatically increase an individual's chances at success or failure. Learn the game plan and blueprint of life and plan the game of life on your own terms.

Words of Gossip Separate Close Friends

October 11, 2023

Gossip or negative talk from a friend can affect the innermost parts of an individual. Evil speech has divided and destroyed families, cultures, and countries. An enemy can disguise themselves with charming speech, but ultimately their hearts harbor deceit. Be wary of speeches of flattery.

~ 288 ~

Wake Up Action Step: From the abundance of the heart, the mouth speaks. One can try to hide their true feelings towards someone, but ultimately people will see and know what's true. Remain true no matter the cost. Even if it may cost you everything, stand up for what's real and true. Truth shall set the people free.

Don't Forsake Your Friends or Family

October 12, 2023

Quitting on someone when they're at a low point in their life, is weak and disgusting. Like a broken tooth or a lame foot relies on the unfaithful in a time of trouble, wounds from a friend can be trusted but an enemy multiplies kisses of deceit.

~ 289 ~

Wake Up Action Step: Stand firm in place for your loved ones. One may never know to what extent an issue has become. Manage expectations when dealing with people. Believe and build with those that are invested. Remain blessed and encouraged.

Don't Boast about Tomorrow

October 13, 2023

No one knows what each day is going to bring. Let someone else praise you, not your own mouth, and not your own lips. Do not answer a fool according to his folly, or he will be wise in his own eyes. Without wood a fire goes out; without a gossip quarrel dies down.

~ 290 ~

Wake Up Action Step: Secure your tomorrow with the work you do today. Work hard, work smart, and work consistently. Increase your chances of success by creating a strategy and reinforcing it with consistent action. Action more and talk less.

Those Who Work Their Land Will Have Abundant Food

October 14, 2023

Those who work their land will have abundant food, but those who chase fantasies may feel poverty. Stop chasing fantasies and chase your goals with a focused plan. Formulate a plan and move towards that direction. Work every day to develop your goals. Be consistent while being focused.

~ 291 ~

Wake Up Action Step: A plan and focused action is one of the surest ways to guarantee success. It's impossible to fail where action and focused work is present. Do the necessary work and enjoy the fruits of your labor. Remain blessed and encouraged.

Where There's No Revelation, People Cast off Restraint

October 15, 2023

Where there is no vision, some people may perish. One important area in leadership is creating and revealing a plan. The rich are wise in their own eyes; one who is poor and discerning sees how deluded they are. Don't trust in your strength alone.

~ *292* ~

Wake Up Action Step: Understand your divine advantage and cultivate your relationship with your source. Those who walk in wisdom are kept safe. Give to the poor. Givers will never lack, but those who close their eyes to the poor could receive many curses.

Truth Detest Dishonesty

October 16, 2023

Where truth is present, lies and dishonest scales will be cleared out. Truth puts a flashlight on everything that's wrong. Whoever rebukes a person will gain favor in the end. The greedy stir up conflict, but those who trust in the Lord will prosper.

~ 293 ~

Wake Up Action Step: The righteous care about the poor, and the mockers stir up a city but turn away anger. Fools bring full vent to their rage, whereas the wise bring calm in the end. Stand by truth irrespective of the consequences. The truth shall set you free.

Fear of Man Will Prove to Be a Snare

October 17, 2023

Trust in the Lord in all your ways, and you will be blessed. Many seek an audience with a ruler, but favor comes from the Lord. The righteous detest the dishonest, and the divisive detest the upright. Fear no man. No one else can do for you, what you can do for yourself.

~ 294 ~

Wake Up Action Step: Man's influence is limited. Connect to the source and turn your life into a resource for yourself and others around you. The fear of the Lord is the beginning of wisdom. Organize your priority and put God first.

Discipline Your Children

October 18, 2023

Disciplining your children will give you peace. Children that are disciplined will bring delight and happiness. When the righteous triumph, there's great elation. However, when the divisive rise to power, people go into hiding. Those who forsake instruction, praise the wicked. By sparing the rod, one has directly abused the child by exposing them to ignorance.

~ 295 ~

Wake Up Action Step: Fall in love with the process. Good things come to those who plan and work. Start working towards the life you deserve today. Use each day as a solidifying force. Brick by brick, day by day each day brings an opportunity for progress.

Every Word of God Is Flawless

October 19, 2023

Every word of God is flawless; He is a shield to those who take refuge. Do not add to His words, or He will rebuke you and prove you to be a liar. May the Lord not refuse you before you die. Keep falsehood and lies far away. Do not seek poverty or riches.

~ 296 ~

Wake Up Action Step: Request for your daily bread and plan accordingly. Pray for the strength to handle what you've been given. Ask for grace for those things that are on the way. Learn to be content with what you have, but also focused on what's on the way. Remain blessed and encouraged.

Speak Up for Those Who Cannot Speak for Themselves

October 20, 2023

Speak up for the rights of all who are destitute, and judge fairly. Defend the rights of the poor and needy. Do not spend your strength chasing after people. Moderate the amount you drink. Charm is deceptive and beauty is fleeting.

~ 297 ~

Wake Up Action Step: Open your arms to the poor and extend your hands to the needy. Fear and praise God. Allow your work to speak the loudest. Actions will always validate or disqualify words.

Work Without Purpose Is Meaningless

October 21, 2023

What do people gain from all their labor? Generations come and generations go, but the earth remains forever. The sun rises and the sun sets, and then rises again. The wind blows to the south and turns to the north. All the streams flow into the sea, yet the sea is never full.

~ *298* ~

Wake Up Action Step: All things are wearisome, more than one can say. The eye never has enough to see or hear. What has been will be again. What has been done will be done again. There is nothing new under the sun.

Chasing after the Wind

October 22, 2023

Apply yourself to studying and exploring wisdom. What a heavy burden that has been placed on people. Many things that are done under the sun are meaningless, chasing after the wind. What is crooked cannot be straightened. What is lacking cannot be counted.

~ 299 ~

Wake Up Action Step: With much wisdom comes much sorrow; the more knowledge, the more grief. Wisdom is better than folly. Light is better than darkness. The wise have eyes in their heads. Fools walk in the darkness.

Chasing after the Wind: Part. 2

October 23, 2023

Ultimately, people's life work will be left to someone that comes after. Who knows whether the person will be wise or foolish? Either way they will have control over all the fruits of a person's toil. A toil in which much effort and skill was exhausted will be controlled and enjoyed by another.

~ 300 ~

Wake Up Action Step: A person may labor with wisdom, knowledge, and skills, and then end up leaving all they own to another individual who has not toiled for it. This is meaningless and a great misfortune. Enjoy your life. Remain blessed and encouraged.

Chasing after the Wind: Part. 3

October 24, 2023

What do people gain for all their toil and anxious striving? All the days of their work is grief and pain. Even at night, their minds are not at rest. A person can do nothing better than to eat and drink and find satisfaction in their toil. Find time for enjoyment. Enjoy your life while you have it. Enjoy your days now.

~ 301 ~

Wake Up Action Step: Please God, for He will grant you wisdom, knowledge, and happiness, but to the divisive, He gives the task of gathering and storing up wealth to hand over to the people He chooses.

A Time for Everything

October 25, 2023

There's a time for everything, and a season for every activity under the heavens. There's a time to be born and a time to die. A time to plant and a time to heal. A time to tear down and a time to laugh. A time to laugh and a time to mourn and dance. A time to scatter stones and a time to gather them. A time to embrace and time to refrain from embracing. A time to search and a time to give up. A time to keep and a time to throw away.

~ 302 ~

Wake Up Action Step: There's a time for every activity under the sun. A time to tear and a time to mend. A time to be silent and a time to speak. A time to love and a time to hate. A time for war and a time for peace. Understand the time and season that you're currently in. Know that no season or time will last forever. Outlast your season. Remain blessed and encouraged.

A Time for Everything: Part. 2

October 26, 2023

There is a time for everything, and a season for every activity under the heavens. What does a worker gain from their toil? There is a burden placed on mankind. He has made everything beautiful in its time. The Almighty has set eternity in the human heart. No one can fathom what God has done from the beginning to end.

~ 303 ~

Wake Up Action Step: There's nothing better than for people to be happy and to do good while they're alive. At the end, each person should eat, drink, and find satisfaction in all their toil. Satisfaction comes from the Lord.

Whatever Is Has Already Been

October 27, 2023

What will be has been before. God will bring into judgment both the good and the bad. There is time for every activity under the sun and there is a time for judgment for every activity. For now, enjoy and embrace your life. There is nothing better for a person to do than enjoy their work.

~ 304 ~

Wake Up Action Step: Who can add a single second to their life by stressing? Pace yourself and remain consistent. Your time is coming! Do the needed work and trust the time of your life. Everything happens as it should and when it should.

Endure Forever

October 28, 2023

Nothing can be added to it, and nothing taken from it. God does it so that people will fear Him. Fear God and trust and fulfill His commandments. No matter how long a person lives, if they can't enjoy their life or have a proper burial, it's perhaps better that they were never born.

~ 305 ~

Wake Up Action Step: Obedience is better than sacrifice. Learn the fundamental principles of success and apply them as soon as possible! Start today to build the life you deserve! Remain blessed and encouraged.

Profits from the Fields

October 29, 2023

Whoever loves money will never be satisfied with their income. Goods increase so do those who consume them. The rich must stay up to protect their wealth. The ability to create wealth and enjoy it, is from God.

~ 306 ~

Wake Up Action Step: Profits from the fields are good, but every good thing comes with responsibility. Appreciate your position but understand everything that comes with it.

The More the Words, the Less the Meaning

October 30, 2023

What does it profit a person to over explain? A good name is better than fine perfume or rare jewelry. It's better to go to the house of the mourning, rather than to the house of the feasting; death is the destiny of everyone. The living should take heart. The day of death is better than the day of birth. It's better to heed the rebuke of a wise person than to listen to the song of fools.

~ 307 ~

Wake Up Action Step: The end of a matter is better than its beginning. Patience is better than pride. Do not be easily provoked in your spirit, for anger resides in the lap of fools. Never think that the old days are better than today. Make the most today and redeem your yesterday.

Wisdom Makes One Person More Powerful

October 31, 2023

Wisdom makes one person more powerful than 10 rulers in a city. A truly righteous person is one void of blemishes, but we all fall short. Don't pay too close attention to every word a person says. You know in your heart that many times, you yourself, have cursed others.

~ 308 ~

Wake Up Action Step: Understanding is like an inheritance. It is good. Wisdom benefits those who are alive to use it. Money and wisdom are like shelters. Wisdom preserves those who have it. Remain blessed and encouraged.

Patience Is Better Than Pride

November 1, 2023

The end of a thing is better than its beginning. Anger resides in the lap of fools. Do not be quickly provoked in your spirit. Nothing on earth is truly guaranteed. The righteous can perish in their righteousness, and the wicked can live long in their wickedness.

~ 309 ~

Wake Up Action Step: Do not be over righteous or overwise. Why destroy yourself? Do not be overwicked and do not be a fool; why die before your time? Do not be foolish, this life is a gift. Treat it as such.

Fear God Not Men

November 2, 2023

Whoever fears God will avoid much harm. Wisdom makes one wise person more powerful than many rulers of a nation. Be determined to be wise. Do not search matters that are too deep. Do your part then leave the rest to God. God created mankind upright, but they have gone in search of many schemes.

~ 310 ~

Wake Up Action Step: A person's wisdom brightens their face and changes its hard appearance. There's a proper time and procedure for every matter, though a person may be weighed down by misery. Remain blessed and encouraged.

No One Knows Tomorrow

November 3, 2023

Who can tell another person what's going to happen tomorrow? No one has the power over the time of their death. No one is discharged in time of war, so the divisive will not escape their own craftiness. Despite all the efforts to search out a thing, there are some things that will never be discovered. There is a common destiny for all. The righteous and the wise are in the hand of the Almighty.

~ 311 ~

Wake Up Action Step: No one knows whether love or hate awaits them. Move with complete confidence. What will be, will be. Good or bad, life is a blessing and a gift either way it comes. Remain blessed and encouraged.

A Common Destiny for All

November 4, 2023

We all share a common destiny. The good, the bad, and the descent will all end up in the same place. The same destiny overtakes all. The living has more hope. A living dog is better than a dead lion. Those living are aware that death awaits them, but the dead know nothing. The dead have no more reward from the living. The name of the dead will be eventually forgotten.

~ 312 ~

Wake Up Action Step: Take heart and remain encouraged. A dead person's love or hate has since passed. Never again can the dead take part in anything under the sun. Eat your food with gladness, and drink with a joyful heart. Enjoy your life and take every opportunity to be at peace.

Whatever Your Hands Find, Do It Well

November 5, 2023

Whatever your hands find to do, do it with all your might. In the realm of the dead, there is neither working, planning or knowledge with wisdom. No one can add a single day to their life by stressing or worrying. Enjoy and embrace your process. Live your life with complete confidence.

~ 313 ~

Wake Up Action Step: The race of life is not for the swift, the crafty or the strong. Food does not come to wise, or wealth to the brilliant, or favor to the educated, but time and chance happens to everyone.

Wisdom Is Better Than Strength

November 6, 2023

The quiet words of the wise are heeded more than a loud fool. A little foolishness weighs much wisdom and honor. Understanding is better than weapons of war. One sinner destroys much good. The heart of the wise tends to live a right life. The heart of the fool tends to live a wrong life. Calmness can lay great offenses to rest.

~ 314 ~

Wake Up Action Step: Fools are placed in many high positions. Always do what's right and good. Never wish anyone evil. Whoever quarries stones may be injured by them. Whoever digs a pit may fall into it. Be good and remain encouraged.

Fools Multiply Words

November 7, 2023

Words from the mouth of the wise are gracious. Fools are consumed by their own words. The beginning of a fool's words is folly and will end in calamity. Choose your words wisely and guard your steps. Take each day one at a time. Each day has enough worry on its own.

~ 315 ~

Wake Up Action Step: No one truly knows what's coming. Do what you can today and plan for the future. Use things and love people. Always speak life. The power of life and death is in the tongue. Choose life, choose purpose. Remain encouraged and blessed.

Skill Will Bring Success

November 8, 2023

Become a master at your craft. Do what you do with a high level of skill and mastery. Generalists are paid for their skill, but specialists can demand more money from the market because of their specialized knowledge. Become an expert in your work and people will seek after you. Never chase money or opportunities. Focus on the value you bring to the marketplace. What's your unique selling point? Create mastery in a specialized niche.

~ 316 ~

Wake Up Action Step: Dominate your niche and increase your price according to the value you can demand. Start today to build out your niche of expertise. You can do it! Start where you are and build from there. Remain encouraged.

Idle Hands Cause the House to Leak

November 9, 2023

Through laziness, the house comes to ruin. Laziness is one of the surest ways to guarantee failure and disappointment. Do not wait for anyone to save you. Create the life you desire. Design what you want in your life. Create a blueprint for your life and run after it as if your life depends on it, because it does. Be careful who you allow in your environment.

~ 317 ~

Wake Up Action Step: Raise the standard through consistent progress and growth. Remove the idea of perfection. Do away with the unnecessary pressure of being perfect. You got this! Remain encouraged, remain blessed.

The Work of The Foolish

November 10, 2023

The work of the foolish may concern some people, and for this reason, they may struggle to succeed in the city. People don't want to build and grow with the foolish. The foolish are consumed by their own lips. In the beginning their words are foolish, and their foolishness is multiplied by many words.

~ 318 ~

Wake Up Action Step: The hands of the foolish may bring harm to themselves and others. Do not curse people in your home. One may carry your thoughts into the public. Manage your time spent with the wise. Go in full confidence.

Money Answers All Things

November 11, 2023

For all problems that are material, money can usually solve them. Is the issue you're dealing with materialistic? If so, money can most likely solve it! Is there a problem that requires monetary resources? Money can solve it. Not all issues are things. There are issues that are larger than things. There are some problems that money cannot fix.

~ 319 ~

Wake Up Action Step: For the issues that require more than just money, creativity must be applied. Think and live outside of the box. Think past what is immediately in front of you. Build up your soul and spirit. Embrace the toughest of times.

Invest In Multiple Ventures

November 12, 2023

Diversify your income and investments. Invest in seven ventures, and if possible, eight. Create opportunities in different parts of the world. Over time you may receive a return on your investment. Whoever watches the wind will not plant; whoever looks at the clouds will not reap. You do not know the path of the wind, or how the body is formed. No one knows or understands the work of God.

~ 320 ~

Wake Up Action Step: Sow your seed in the morning, and in the evening let your hands not be idle. Life is a game of time, chance, and probability. By investing in many ventures, you dramatically increase your chance of sustained success. Start investing today. Remain encouraged and stay blessed.

Remember Your Creator

November 13, 2023

Remember your creator while you're young. No matter the number of years a person is alive on earth, be sure to enjoy them all. Light is sweet and pleases the eyes to see the sun. Remember the creator in the days of darkness, for there will be many. Avoid meaningless things at all costs. Work to build the life you deserve. Take time to create a game plan for life.

~ 321 ~

Wake Up Action Step: Enjoy your youth and be happy while you're young. Allow your heart to give you joy in the days of your youth. Follow the ways of your heart. Know that for all things, God will bring you into judgment. Release anxiety from your heart and remove the troubles of your body. Worrying is meaningless and adds no true value. Take heart and remain encouraged. Your time has arrived. Remain blessed and encouraged.

Remember Your Creator: Part 2

November 14, 2023

Remember your creator while you're young. Before the days of trouble come, remember your creator. The time will come when things that are valued will no longer be important. People go to their eternal home and mourners go about the streets. Remember Him before the silver cord is severed. What you put in, is what you receive.

~ *322* ~

Wake Up Action Step: Give credit where credit is due. Understand where you fit in and maximize your position. Take what you've been given and turn it into something of value and dignity. Take pride in finishing. Remain encouraged in all that you do.

The Conclusion

November 15, 2023

The teacher is wise and imparts knowledge to the people. He searched out and set in order many truths. The teacher searched to find just the right words, and what was written is upright and true. The words of the wise are like matches. Collected wisdom opens the path of success and prosperity. Never add to or remove from the words of truth. There is no end to books and study. Don't exhaust yourself by over studying and reading.

~ 323 ~

Wake Up Action Step: Everything has been spoken and written. Fear God and keep His commandments, for this is the duty of all mankind. For God will bring every deed into judgment. Whether good or bad, God is the ultimate judge. Remain encouraged and blessed.

Do What Is Right

November 16, 2023

Do what is right and what is just. Do not seek rewards for fulfilling principles. Every true principle contains truths that are consistent. Give prudence your ways and steps. Think through who you would like to become. Calculate how much energy and effort is needed to accomplish and arrive at the desired destination.

~ 324 ~

Wake Up Action Step: Let the discerning receive guidance for their understanding. The fear of the Lord is the beginning of knowledge, but fools despise wisdom and instruction. Add to your learning daily. Invest in material and information that can improve you in a positive and encouraging way.

Be Wise and Take Action

November 17, 2023

Learning and knowing information is not enough to be successful. Applying the correct information at the right time can save and improve your life. When calamity and disaster overtake you like a storm, you need to apply the right information to overcome difficult times. During difficult times, knowing what to do is not enough to be successful.

~ 325 ~

Wake Up Action Step: One must apply the correct information to see and experience tangible results. Store up the commands and wisdoms inside of you. Turn your ears to wisdom and apply your mind to understanding and application. Start today and take action. Remain encouraged and blessed.

Hidden Treasures

November 18, 2023

Hidden treasures are stored inside of wisdom and understanding. Embrace your process. With every problem and conflict there is a hidden opportunity. Find God and knowledge and wisdom will find you. Success is in store for the upright. It's a shield to those whose walk is blameless. The Almighty guards the course of the just and protects the way of the faithful. Through your applications of these principles, you will understand what is right and what is just.

~ 326 ~

Wake Up Action Step: Every good path begins with faith and belief. One must exercise the proper faith to execute and take advantage of hidden truths. Start today to build out who you are. Build your belief system through applying the correct principles over an extended period of time. Begin today and work out your faith. Remain encouraged and stay blessed.

Discretion Protects

November 19, 2023

Discretion will protect you and understanding will guard you. Wisdom will save you from the ways of divisive people. Divisive men who are pervasive have left the right path to walk in the ways of the crooked. Wisdom will save you from the wrong people. Those who follow the way of the dead will miss the path of life.

~ 327 ~

Wake Up Action Step: Walk in the way of the good and keep the paths of the righteous, for the upright will live and dominate the land. The division will be cut off from the land. The faithful will be torn from it. Remain encouraged and blessed.

Let Love and Faithfulness Never Leave You

November 20, 2023

Do not forget the teachings of God and keep the commandments in your heart. Application of truth will prolong your life many years and bring you peace and prosperity. Write truth on the tablet of your heart. By doing this, you will win favor and a good name in the sight of God and man.

~ 328 ~

Wake Up Action Step: "Trust in the Lord with all your heart and lean not on your own understanding. In all your ways submit to him, and he will make your paths straight." (Prv 3:5-6 NIV). Take heart and be at peace. Following life's laws and principles will give you peace of mind above all understanding. Remain encouraged and blessed.

Honor The Lord with Your Wealth

November 21, 2023

Honor the Lord with the first fruits of all your crops. By doing so, your barns will overflow, and your vats will brim over with new wine. Do not be wise in your own eyes. Fear the Lord and reject evil. Do not despise the Lord's discipline, and do not resent his rebuke. The Lord disciplines those He loves, just as a father delight in his son.

~ 329 ~

Wake Up Action Step: Those who find wisdom and understanding are blessed. Wisdom is more profitable than silver and yields better returns than gold. It is more precious than rubies. Nothing you desire can compare with it. Wisdom yields long life. Riches and honor are with everyone who practices these principles. Remain encouraged and blessed.

A Tree of Life

November 22, 2023

Wisdom is more profitable silver and/or gold. Through God's wisdom and understanding, the earth's foundation was established, and everything was put in place. With His knowledge, the watery depths were divided. Do not let wisdom and understanding out of your sight. Preserve sound judgment and discretion; it can lift your life and serve as an ornament that will grace your neck. If you follow these principles, you will be on your way to safety, and your feet will not stumble.

~ 330 ~

Wake Up Action Step: Have no fear of sudden disaster or ruin that overtakes the divisive. "If God is for [you], who can be against [you]?" (Rom 8:31 NIV). Remain encouraged for the Almighty will keep and protect you in all your ways.

The Wise Inherit Honor

November 23, 2023

Do not withhold good from those to whom it's due. When it's within your power, give to those who are in need. Do not plot evil against yourself or those who are around you. Be careful about who you accuse. The same accusations you bring could be used against you. Be slow to speak and quick to observe. The Almighty blesses the home of the righteous.

~ 331 ~

Wake Up Action Step: An investment in wisdom pays off continuously. Search for wisdom even if it costs you everything you have. Wisdom will protect and provide in due time. Remain blessed and encouraged.

Wisdom at Any Cost

November 24, 2023

Pay attention, gain understanding, and give to sound learning. Don't forsake fundamental teachings; these teachings will watch over you. The beginning of wisdom is to attain it. Invest everything to gain understanding. Cherish and appreciate becoming knowledgeable, it will prosper and elevate you. Accepting these truths for applications of principles will add years to your life. The Lord instructs in the way of wisdom.

~ 332 ~

Wake Up Action Step: Pay attention to the words of the wise. Don't let the words leave you. Don't allow the words to forsake you. Keep these truths deep inside the tablet of your heart. This is life to those who find it, and health to one's whole body.

Free Yourself

November 25, 2023

Live your life and free yourself. Don't put up security for your neighbor. Be careful when shaking the hands of a strangers. Don't be trapped by what you say but be wise and avoid being ensnared by the words of your mouth. Free yourself, when trapped by your neighbor's hands. Go to the point of exhaustion and give your neighbor no rest!

~ 333 ~

Wake Up Action Step: Allow no sleep or rest until you've been fully liberated from injustice. Protect yourself by any cost. Your life matters, so protect it with everything that you own. Build out the life you deserve. Remain blessed and encouraged.

A Little Sleep and a Little Slumber

November 26, 2023

The wise store their provisions in the summer and gather their food at harvest. How long will you wait and hope without a plan of action? The most dangerous position in life is a life without action and movement. To stay in the same position is to go backwards. A little folding of the hands to rest and poverty will jump on you like a thief at night. Scarcity and lack is behind complacency and laxity.

~ 334 ~

Wake Up Action Step: Disaster will overtake a divisive and corrupt mouth. Remain focused and determined in every situation. Visualize your destination and lock in with phenomenal action and follow through. Remain blessed and encouraged.

Seven Seeds of Discord

November 27, 2023

There are seven seeds of discord that divide. A prideful heart and spirit divides. A lying tongue and hands that shed innocent blood and seeks to separate. A divisive heart filled with evil intent, and feet that are quick to rush to do wrong will end in division.

~ 335 ~

Wake Up Action Step: A false witness who pours out lies and a person who creates conflict in the community should be avoided and managed to keep peace in the community. Use wisdom and care when you see such behaviors. These character traits seek to kill, steal, and destroy. Choose peace and love. Remain encouraged and blessed.

Speak What Is True

November 28, 2023

Do not allow your lips to speak lies. Stay away from crooked and perverse speech. Choose instruction and knowledge over silver and/or gold. Wisdom is more precious than jewelry. Nothing on earth can compare to goodness and sound truth. Possess and maintain knowledge and discretion.

~ 336 ~

Wake Up Action Step: Fear God and shun what is evil. Avoid pride and arrogance at all costs. Maintain counsel and sound judgment. Develop good insight and create power. Through wisdom, kings reign, and princes govern.

Love Those Who Love You

November 29, 2023

Those who seek truth will find it. Wisdom keeps riches and honor. Enduring wealth and prosperity are available for all those who seek wisdom and understanding. Wisdom and understanding will do more for you than physical wealth. Wisdom can create the wealth, but applied understanding is needed to maintain and build wealth over time.

~ 337 ~

Wake Up Action Step: Love more and hate less. Love creates the necessary energy to accomplish success. Decide each day to love yourself. Even if you are not where you would like to be in life, know and understand that great things require a process. In due time it will work out the way it's supposed to - with love and care. Remain encouraged and blessed.

Keep the Ways of the Lord

November 30, 2023

Those who keep and maintain the ways of the Lord are blessed. Listen and apply instruction in all your ways. Be wise and productive. No one knows how much time they are allotted on planet earth. Leverage the wisdom you've been given. Seek truth everyday of life.

~ 338 ~

Wake Up Action Step: Those who find the ways of the Lord, will find life, and receive favor from the Almighty. Those who don't, may find failure and bring grief upon themselves. Those who hate truth, love death. Choose truth and choose life, for this is wise. Remain encouraged and blessed.

Wisdom Builds a House

December 1, 2023

Wisdom has set up its seven pillars. It has prepared a table in the presence of her (wisdom) enemies. Wisdom seats one apart. Those who are simple in their ways should find wisdom and understanding. To those who have no sense can seek and find her (wisdom). For the jewels of wisdom will bring light and shine into their life.

~ 339 ~

Wake Up Action Step: The benefits of wisdom will make a way. Never underestimate the power of persistent and consistent applied wisdom. Over time the difference is clear. Stay the course and remain on the path of peace and progression. Remain encouraged and blessed.

Whoever Rebukes the Wicked Incurs Abuse

December 2, 2023

Trying to educate someone who's not interested in self-improvement is a waste of time. The most expensive expense is ignorance because it can cost you everything. Do not rebuke mockers, they will hate you. Rebuke the wise, they will love you. Instruct the wise and they will become wiser.

~ 340 ~

Wake Up Action Step: Teach the righteous and their knowledge will increase. The fear of the Lord is the beginning of wisdom. The knowledge of the Holy One is understanding. Continue to develop and improve yourself. Remain encouraged and blessed.

Years Will Be Added to Your Life

December 3, 2023

Through wisdom, days will be added to your life. If you're wise, your wisdom will reward you. If you're a mocker, you alone will suffer. Ignorance is a liability. It's simple and knows nothing. A wise son brings joy to his father, but a foolish son brings grief to his mother. Ill-gotten treasures have no lasting value, but righteousness delivers from death.

~ 341 ~

Wake Up Action Step: The [Almighty] does not let the righteous go hungry, but he thwarts the craving of the wicked." (Prov 10:3 NIV). Givers can never be beggars. The meek shall inherit the earth and everything within it. Remain encouraged and blessed.

Avoid Lazy Hands

December 4, 2023

Ill-gotten riches have no lasting value. Lazy hands make for poverty and lack. One way to guarantee failure is by becoming lazy and complacent. Laziness looks to steal, kill, and destroy. A friend to one that is slack in their work is a friend to one who could kill. Avoid lazy hands by all costs and measures. Work your fields until they yield profit.

~ 342 ~

Wake Up Action Step: Out work the work. Work smarter but be consistent and persistent in all that you do. Remain encouraged and blessed.

Be Diligent in All of Your Ways

December 5, 2023

Work to self-improve constantly. Those who gather crops in the summer are prudent and wise. Those who sleep during the time, in which they should be working and building, will only disgrace themselves. There is a time and place and for everything. Plan when it's time to plan, work when it's time to work, and build when it's time to build. Understand and utilize your time appropriately.

~ 343 ~

Wake Up Action Step: Blessings crown the head of those who are righteous. Do what is right even when it may not be beneficial. Start building where you are. Even if you aren't where you would like to be, be consistent and follow through with your actions. Remain encouraged and blessed.

Blessings Crown the Head of the Righteous

December 6, 2023

Violence will overtake the mouth of the wicked. The wise will accept commands, but a talkative fool will soon come to ruin. Whoever walks in the counsel of the wise will too become wise. Be careful who you spend your time with. You become what you invest your time into.

~ 344 ~

Wake Up Action Step: If you want a better life, invest into activities that will improve you in that area. Work into progression. Whoever walks in wisdom and understanding is forever protected and guided. Remain blessed and encouraged.

The Love of God

December 7, 2023

There is nothing more powerful on planet earth than the love of God. Nothing can stop the love God. Neither death or life, neither angels or demons, neither the present nor the future, nor any powers, neither height nor depth, nor anything else in all creation, will be able to separate you from the love of God. Nothing is bad enough to stop you from developing an authentic relation with the Almighty God.

~ 345 ~

Wake Up Action Step: Just start building a relationship with God no matter where you are spiritually. Even if you're in dark place, remain encouraged. Don't wait to be perfect to build a relationship; build a relationship and wait for the Almighty to perfect your ways. Start today where you are at no matter where you stand.

New Every Morning

December 8, 2023

The Lord's mercies are new every morning. The steadfast love of the Lord never ceases. His mercies never come to an end. Great is the faithfulness of God. No matter the situation or the problem you're currently facing, the sun will still shine. The morning will still come.

~ 346 ~

Wake Up Action Step: Be strong and firm in all your actions. The morning represents new opportunities and new seasons. Move through your day with full confidence and belief. Stay encouraged and blessed.

Do Not Lose Heart

December 9, 2023

Build up your faith daily. Nothing outside can sink your ship inside unless you allow it. Though our outer self is wasting away, our inner self is being renewed day by day. Even though you may go through a difficult time, there is always light at the end of the tunnel.

~ 347 ~

Wake Up Action Step: The light of momentary affliction is preparing us an eternal weight of glory beyond all comparison, as we look to things not seen, but to the things that are seen. Remain encouraged and blessed.

Do Immeasurably More Than

December 10, 2023

"Now to him who is able to do immeasurably more than all we ask or imagine, according to his power that is at work within us." (Eph 3:20 NIV). Learn to encourage yourself. You are worth your belief. You are worth everything that is good. Build and develop your faith. Everything is predicated on the strength of your faith.

~ 348 ~

Wake Up Action Step: Look where you are at today. What role did you play to get where you're at today? Take full responsibility. The only way to move forward is by measuring where you come from. Remain encouraged and blessed.

Have No Fear

December 11, 2023

May the God of hope fill you with all joy and peace as you trust in Him. May you overflow with hope by the power of the Holy Spirit. Cast away all fears. Be strong and courageous. Relying on God enables us to be productive and sacrifice for others.

~ 349 ~

Wake Up Action Step: Love protects us from fear and makes us stronger. Leverage wisdom on the days that are difficult. No season lasts forever. Remain encouraged and blessed.

Be Strong and Courageous

December 12, 2023

Always be strong and courageous. Don't be afraid or terrified because the Lord your God goes with you. He will never leave you, nor forsake you. Life may throw a curve ball your way, but you must stand strong in the face of adversity. Stay consistent and never cower. God makes a way for His own.

~ *350* ~

Wake Up Action Step: Remain encouraged and blessed. You are covered in all your ways. Progression and advancement are necessary. Keep swinging at your target. Your time is right in front of you. Be sure to grab your opportunity when it's time.

The Lord Is My Stronghold

December 13, 2023

"The Lord is my light and my salvation – whom shall I fear? The Lord is the stronghold of my life – of whom shall I be afraid?" (Ps 27:1 NIV). Fear God and everything else will work itself out. Build strong faith through strong execution and follow through.

~ 351 ~

Wake Up Action Step: Understanding and leveraging time is best way to create and predict the future you desire and deserve. Start building out the future you would like to see today. Take each season as it is and embrace the moment. Redeem your time here on earth. Remain blessed and encouraged.

Perfect Love Drives Out Fear

December 14, 2023

Fear and faith cannot operate together. You must choose one over the other. Perfect love builds up faith and trust. The one who fears is not made perfect in love. Take today to develop your faith through lovely and faithful actions. Work to move from fear to faith. Take one step at a time.

~ 352 ~

Wake Up Action Step: Do not overwhelm yourself. Commit to a pace you can manage and grow. Once you find the right speed for you, follow through as is if your life depends on it, because it does. Remain blessed and encouraged.

God Is for You

December 15, 2023

Take heart and understand you can do all things through the strength of the Almighty. Personal belief and faith can take you further than you can imagine. Every great concept and idea start with faith. It takes faith to move an idea to reality. If God is for us, who can be against us? The answer is no one. One can't successfully go against the word of God.

~ 353 ~

Wake Up Action Step: Develop and grow consistently. The most important relationship is between yourself and God. The better you know yourself, the better you can relate with others. Start building today!

Let Your Heart Take Courage

December 16, 2023

No matter the opposition, let your heart take courage. Remain encouraged and be willing to bet everything on yourself. You can only go as far as your faith. Be strong and let your heart take courage. Wait on the Lord! Patience is a virtue. Adversity builds character, and time cures all.

~ 354 ~

Wake Up Action Step: With persistence, you can overcome resistance. Take control of your life and understand what's within your control and what's not. Remain encouraged and blessed.

Faith More and Fear Less

December 17, 2023

Fear not, for the Almighty is with you. Fear does not fulfill your purpose. Fear is one of the biggest stumbling blocks to achieving your purpose. Fear and faith cannot operate together. Choose which master you want to serve. Do not fear, God is with you. If the Almighty is with you, who be against you?

~ 355 ~

Wake Up Action Step: Be in full confidence that a better is coming. Take ownership of who you are, and where you're positioned be. The sun will eventually shine again. Tough times don't last, but tough people do. Remain encouraged and take heart.

Greater Love Has No One Than This

December 18, 2023

Greater love has no one than this: to lay down one's life for one's friends. There are different definitions of love. True love is qualified through action. Love is sacrifice. What greater sacrifice can one friend do for another that's greater than life? Appreciate your loved ones while they're alive.

~ 356 ~

Wake Up Action Step: Don't wait to express and show love to your loved ones. Tomorrow is not guaranteed, so take every opportunity to extend gratitude to those who matter to you the most. Remain encouraged and blessed.

Anything Is Possible

December 19, 2023

Truly all things are possible. If you're discouraged or feeling hopeless, a brighter tomorrow is in front of you. Connect with your Creator. By building a relationship with your source you can build your faith, confidence, and motivation. The Almighty provides strength in every area of your life. Be encouraged and know your tomorrow is blessed and secured.

~ 357 ~

Wake Up Action Step: Who can secure you more than the ultimate Creator? No amount of security can secure you more than building and investing in your relationship with God. Remain encouraged and blessed.

All Things Are Possible with God

December 20, 2023

All things are possible with God. Never limit your belief based on other people's opinion. No one truly knows and understand your life's purpose and potential more than yourself and your God. Take time to meditate and focus on yourself. Where would you like to be in 10 years? How do you see your life progressing in the future?

~ 358 ~

Wake Up Action Step: Ask yourself these questions every day. Be honest with yourself and your responses. Do the necessary work and build towards the future. Start where you are. Remain encouraged and blessed.

With Man This Is Impossible

December 21, 2023

Never put your full trust into people because naturally people can only give you what they have. Go directly to the source, God. Direct your time and energy directly to the source. Partner and build with the ultimate builder.

~ 359 ~

Wake Up Action Step: Humans are resources, which means there's an original source. Connect to the original source and your whole life will improve dramatically. Start to build out the life you deserve today. Remain encouraged and blessed.

You Can Do All Things Through Him

December 22, 2023

Know and understand where your strength comes from. Most physical manifestations originate from the spiritual relm. Do not depend on people. People will eventually fail you or let you down. Take people for who they are and leave the rest to God; He will sort it out.

~ 360 ~

Wake Up Action Step: Leave the rest to God and take solace that the Creator has the last word. All things can be accomplished through Him. Build yourself up to know and accept this truth. Remain encouraged and blessed.

Faith Provides Strength

December 23, 2023

One key to increasing personal strength is improving personal faith. Your faith is directly tied to your internal strength. When your faith in God is weak, it's essential to remind yourself of God's love. Remembering God's love will make us stronger and will help refocus our energy to what's truly important.

~ 361 ~

Wake Up Action Step: The right work that we sacrifice is appreciated by our Creator. Faith and trust are the foundation of love. Stay the course. Finish your race! Remain encouraged and blessed.

In The Lord Your Labor Is Not in Vain

December 24, 2023

The right work you do is important and necessary to this world. Be steadfast, immovable, and always abounding in the work of the Lord, knowing that in the Lord, your labor is not in vain. Make sure your work aligns with your purpose. What a waste it would be to come to the end of your life only to realize you were in the wrong work and ministry.

~ 362 ~

Wake Up Action Step: Ask yourself the important questions about your life as soon as possible. You owe yourself the truth. You owe yourself the highest version of yourself. Be kind to yourself. Remain encouraged and blessed.

Do Not Lean on Your Own Understanding

December 25, 2023

Be careful depending on your own understanding. Our understanding is limited and restricted. Consult with the Creator for original information. "Trust in the Lord with all your heart. In all your ways acknowledge Him, and He will make your paths straight." (Prv 3: 5-6 BSB).

~ 363 ~

Wake Up Action Step: Take it one day at a time. Your day will surely come to past. Work to grow every day of your life. Never depend on another man or woman. Don't make yourself foolish and don't be fooled. The responsibility of success rests solely on the shoulders of the individual. Take heart for your time is coming. Remain encouraged and blessed.

Stand Firm in the Faith

December 26, 2023

Remain strong and stand for what's right. Be watchful and stand firm in your faith. Do everything with love. You are responsible for the energy you give to the world. Take full ownership of your non-verbal communication.

~ 364 ~

Wake Up Action Step: People are affected more by the energy you give off. Words are only as powerful as the actions that follow. Encourage and motivate yourself. There's no guarantee anyone will do the work for you. Remain encouraged and blessed.

Our Faith Can Move Mountains

December 27, 2023

Celebrate God's love. Appreciating and celebrating God's love will energize and strengthen us while at the same time, renewing our faith. God's goodness is shown in people's lives daily. The source of our strength is found in loving God. The best way to have the life you desire and deserve is to create the reality that you see.

~ 365 ~

Wake Up Action Step: Create a plan, work each day to achieve your daily goals, and love God and others. Embrace your process. Your timing is perfect. Everything that happens was predestined and written before time. Remain encouraged and blessed.

Love Endures Forever

December 28, 2023

What's real will stand the test of time. Give thanks to the Lord, for He is good. His love endures forever. The Lord knows the plans He has for you. The Almighty has plans to prosper you and not harm you. He has plans to give you hope, a future, and an expected end.

~ 366 ~

Wake Up Action Step: Love conquers all. Move in love and understand that only truth and love will remain. Remain encouraged and blessed.

All Things Work for the Good of Those Who Trust in the Lord

December 29, 2023

Good people will always win in the end. God favors those who love Him and follow His commandments. Taste and see that the Lord is good. Blessed is the one who takes refuge in Him.

~ 367 ~

Wake Up Action Step: All things work for the good of those who love Him and have been called according to His purpose. Do the work, but never underestimate the power of divine favor and grace. Grace is not something you can pay for or merit. When God graces your life, walk fully into your blessings. Remain encouraged and blessed.

Rejoice in the Lord

December 30, 2023

Eat good foods and sweet drinks. Give to those who are not able. Enjoy and celebrate every day, in which you're given. Even if you're having a character-building day, celebrate the fact you were able to wake up. There are people in the hospital right now who may be praying to take one more extra breath. If you have air in your lungs, you should give thanks and praise.

~ 368 ~

Wake Up Action Step: Life is amazingly beautiful and is changing and expanding each day. Take life for what it is and understand the biggest and most impactful change must occur inside. Remain encouraged and blessed.

Sing to the Lord a New Song

December 31, 2023

Each day you wake up, have joy and gratitude because tomorrow is not guaranteed. Thank God you were able to wake up. The life you live is not your own. You were given life by the Lord Almighty. Take ownership of the fact that your life is not your own. You were created for a specific purpose. Sing to the Lord, all the earth. Sing to the Lord and praise His name. Uplift and praise His name every day. Declare His glory among the nations.

~ 369 ~

Wake Up Action Step: Understand and appreciate the role you play. Remain encouraged throughout each season of life. There is no permanent season. All things that start must eventually end. Remain blessed in every area of your life.

Called According to Purpose

Taste and see that the Lord is good. Blessed is the one who takes refuge in the Lord. God works all things for the good of those who love and are called according to His purpose. What is God's purpose for your life? This is a question that must be asked to maximize purpose and time while on earth. We are given a specific amount of time on earth to find and fulfill purpose.

~ 370 ~

Wake Up Action Step: We are on a race against time to accomplish our life's purpose and find and finish our life's work. Move in complete confidence for your Lord is your strength. Remain encouraged and blessed.

Do Not Be Saddened

No matter the situation be of great hope and courage. You can overcome any situation in front of you. Eat and drink good food. Give to those that don't have. Rejoice fully in the Lord for He is your strength. When life becomes a bit more challenging, speak to God.

~ 371 ~

Wake Up Action Step: God hears you and He will never forsake you. He is your ultimate comforter in times of trouble. The Lord loves you and will keep you safe. Do not be anxious or sad. Remain encouraged and blessed.

The Lord Cares for You

No matter what you're currently going through, the Lord cares. He cares about every detail of your life. He cares about you in ways you may not know or understand. Cast all your anxieties on Him. He cares for you. The fear of man will prove to be a snare.

~ 372 ~

Wake Up Action Step: Whoever trusts in the Lord is kept safe. As a mother comforts her child, so will the Lord comfort you. You are loved, appreciated, and cared for. Go in complete confidence. May the God Almighty continue to bless and uphold you.

ABOUT THE AUTHOR

Casey Chinedu Ifedi is a licensed Realtor and Property Manager in the state of North Carolina. From student housing, real estate consultation and real estate investing; both professionally and personally, Mr. Ifedi works with clients to create a practical and holistic real estate strategy. While a student at ECU, Casey was able to create The T.E.A.M., which created open dialogue between students and faculty in improving and enhancing the on-campus experience.

Email: theteamhousing@gmail.com / #704-301-8399 / IG: C.Ifedi / Facebook: GenChinedu

www.ingramcontent.com/pod-product-compliance
Lightning Source LLC
Chambersburg PA
CBHW060116200326
41518CB00008B/833